O9-AIG-742

CELLS
THE BUILDING BLOCKS OF LIFE

Cells and Human Health

Cells: The Building Blocks of Life

Cells and Human Health

Cell Structure, Processes, and Reproduction

The Evolution of Cells

How Scientists Research Cells

Plant Cells

Stem Cell Research and Other Cell-Related Controversies

CELLS
THE BUILDING BLOCKS OF LIFE

Cells and Human Health

INGRID SCHAEFER SPRAGUE

CHELSEA HOUSE
An Infobase Learning Company

Cells and Human Health

Copyright © 2012 by Infobase Learning

Chelsea House
An imprint of Infobase Learning
132 West 31st Street
New York NY 10001

Library of Congress Cataloging-in-Publication Data
Sprague, Ingrid Schaefer.
  Cells and human health / by Ingrid Schaefer Sprague.
    p. cm. — (Cells, the building blocks of life)
  Includes bibliographical references and index.
  ISBN 978-1-61753-008-1 (hardcover)
  1. Cells—Popular works. 2. Health—Popular works. I. Title.
  QH582.4.S67 2011
  611'.0181—dc23   2011013253

Chelsea House books are available at special discounts when purchased in bulk quantities for businesses, associations, institutions, or sales promotions. Please call our Special Sales Department in New York at (212) 967-8800 or (800) 322-8755.

You can find Chelsea House on the World Wide Web at http://www.infobaselearning.com

Text design by Erika K. Arroyo
Cover design by Alicia Post
Composition by EJB Publishing Services
Cover printed by IBT Global, Troy, N.Y.
Book printed and bound by IBT Global, Troy, N.Y.
Date printed: November 2011
Printed in the United States of America

10 9 8 7 6 5 4 3 2 1

This book is printed on acid-free paper.

All links and Web addresses were checked and verified to be correct at the time of publication. Because of the dynamic nature of the Web, some addresses and links may have changed since publication and may no longer be valid.

On the cover: A human cancer cell

Contents

• • •

1 The Role of Cells in Human Health   7

2 Cytology: The History of Cell Study
and Its Effects on Human Health   23

3 How Cells Work Together   36

4 Immunity: Defending the Cell   49

5 Unseen Enemies: Bacterial, Viral,
Fungal, and Parasitic Threats   65

6 Genetics: When "Family Traditions"
Can Be Harmful   78

7 Modern Scourges: The Threats
of Cancer and HIV/AIDS   91

8 Cell Repair, Replacement, and Death   100

Glossary   106

Bibliography   119

Further Resources   121

Picture Credits   123

Index   124

About the Author, Dedication and
Acknowledgment   130

The Role of Cells in Human Health: What is a Cell?

Almost anyone can distinguish a living organism from a nonliving, or inanimate, object. But what is life? As humans, we have superior knowledge that enables us to discuss the scientific, philosophical, and theological concepts about life and to consider its origin, meaning, and purpose. Scientists seek to identify and understand the characteristics of life that are defined by theories derived from scientific experiments and observations. Shortly after **cells** were discovered with the use of a microscope, the **cell theory** was proposed, which states that all organisms are composed of cells, and all cells are produced by other cells. Whether it is human, plant, animal, or bacteria, the cell is the basic building block of all living organisms.

TYPES OF CELLS

All life is sustained by the activities carried out in the cell. Cells can be either eukaryotic or prokaryotic. **Eukaryotic cells** are found in plants, animals, protists, and fungi. Humans are multicellular organisms comprised of highly specialized eukaryotic cells. To survive, humans maintain their energy needs by consuming plants, animals, and fungi that consist of eukaryotic cells. Eukaryotic cells range in size from 2 microns (μm), the size of a human **sperm** cell, to 100 μm, the size of a human **ovum** (egg). (One thousand microns equals 1 millimeter.) The size of a human

(continues on page 10)

WHERE DID THE FIRST LIVING CELL COME FROM?

There are several scientific theories about the origin of life. In 2010, world-renowned physicist Stephen Hawking publicly supported the notion of spontaneous generation of life. Even though this idea was proposed before 2010, it remains a hotbed of debate, predominantly because of creationism (the belief that the universe and life were created by God or a higher power). Another possible source of life on Earth is that it had an extraterrestrial origin. Known as the *panspermia theory*, this idea proposes that meteors or other cosmic dust may have brought organic molecules to our planet. However, unlike these concepts, spontaneous generation theorizes that organic chemicals arose spontaneously to become the building blocks of life. Over time, the organic molecules that formed became more stable and developed complex associations. Where exactly life started is also a controversial topic among scientists who debate whether life began at the ocean's edge, under frozen oceans, deep in the earth's crust, within clay, or at deep-sea vents.

Although we do not know when the first cells appeared on Earth, we do know that the earliest cells were prokaryotic cells that obtained necessary organic molecules from the environment. When the amount of oxygen increased in the atmosphere, certain anaerobic organisms (meaning those that didn't use oxygen) adapted to develop respiratory pathways to obtain more energy from food. It is believed that eukaryotic cells of plants, animals, fungi, and protists descended from simpler prokaryotic cells. According to endosymbiotic theory, the chloroplasts and mitochondria found in eukaryotes developed from various bacteria incorporated into the prokaryotic cell. Our earliest records of life date back to fossils of bacteria that are 3.5 billion years old.

Opposite: Figure 1.1 The endosymbiotic theory notes that the mitochondria and chloroplasts in eukaryotic cells originated from bacteria incorporated into a prokaryotic cell.

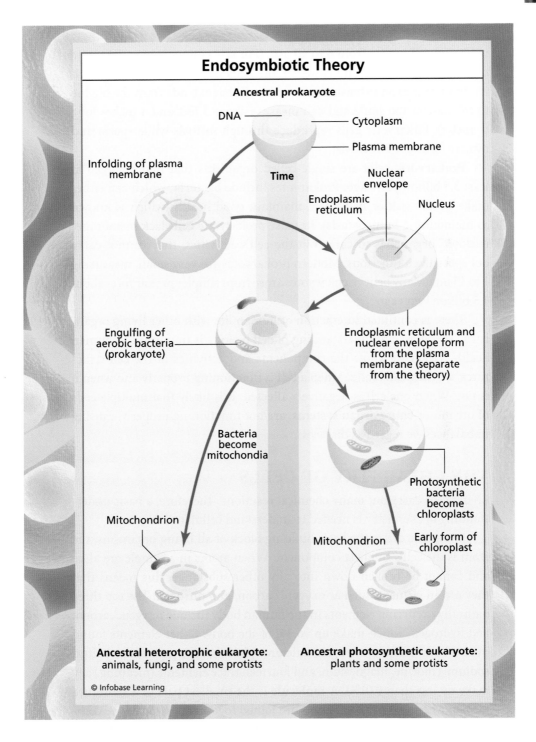

Endosymbiotic Theory

Ancestral prokaryote

DNA —————————— Cytoplasm

————————— Plasma membrane

Infolding of plasma membrane

Time

Nuclear envelope

Endoplasmic reticulum

Nucleus

Engulfing of aerobic bacteria (prokaryote)

Endoplasmic reticulum and nuclear envelope form from the plasma membrane (separate from the theory)

Bacteria become mitochondia

Photosynthetic bacteria become chloroplasts

Mitochondrion

Mitochondrion

Early form of chloroplast

Ancestral heterotrophic eukaryote: animals, fungi, and some protists

Ancestral photosynthetic eukaryote: plants and some protists

© Infobase Learning

(*continued from page 7*)

red blood cell ranges from 6 to 10 μm. (For size comparison, a dust mite measures around 400 μm.) However, the longest neuron in the body with its significant axon extension is a nerve cell that extends from the big toe to the base of the spine and can measure about 3 feet and 4 inches long (1 meter). Eukaryotic cells reproduce through **mitosis** while sperm and ova are formed via **meiosis.**

Prokaryotic cells are single-celled organisms that first emerged at least 3.5 billion years ago. Prokaryotes include **bacteria**, which can either make people sick or help them maintain good health (which is known as maintaining **homeostasis**). Because prokaryotic cells lack membrane-enclosed **organelles** to carry out the cell's activities, they cannot carry out specialized functions. Modern prokaryotes are very small, measuring 1 to 15 μm. Many believe eukaryotes arose from simpler prokaryotes about 1.5 billion years ago.

There is continual interaction of human life with other living organisms. Therefore, an understanding of cell biology is important to human health. When we know the components and activities of the cell structures, we then can realize when a cell is functioning properly and when it is not. When one cell is negatively affected, it is likely that multiple cells of organs, or entire **organ systems**, are not functioning properly, causing imbalances we regard as diseases.

THE CHEMISTRY OF CELLS

Living cells carry out many chemical reactions. Therefore, a basic understanding of chemistry is needed to understand cellular biology.

Just as the cell is the basic building block of all living organisms, the atom is the cell's smallest component. When atoms in a sample are alike and cannot be broken down into any other substance, this means that they are an element, such as oxygen, carbon, and nitrogen. The top three naturally occurring elements in the human body include oxygen, carbon, and hydrogen, which make up 96.3% of the body. Other elements found in the body include nitrogen, calcium, phosphorus, potassium, sulfur, sodium, chlorine, magnesium, and fourteen trace elements (meaning they make up less than 0.01%). A **molecule** is the smallest part of a substance formed when two or more atoms are joined together chemically. A compound is formed from two or more different elements. (Thus, as we can see, all compounds are molecules, but not all molecules are compounds.)

Most of the body's molecules are organic compounds. That means they include carbon atoms that are covalently bonded to form the backbone of the compound. The body contains a huge number of macromolecules. These are large molecules that are built from small organic compounds linked together in chains.

The macromolecules found in living organisms include carbohydrates, lipids, proteins, and nucleic acids. **Carbohydrates** are used by cells to store energy and provide support. These organic compounds include sugars, starches, celluloses, and gums. **Lipids** store energy and provide the structure of cell membranes. This class of organic compounds includes fats, waxes, and oils, and cannot be dissolved in water. **Proteins** are involved in many cellular activities, including providing structure (for example, to your hair and in collagen), assisting in chemical reactions (by way of **enzymes**), and functioning as **hormones** and **neurotransmitters**. The building blocks of proteins are **amino acids.** Another important group of macromolecules are **nucleic acids**, which house the cell's hereditary information. The small repeating unit of a nucleic acid is called a nucleotide; it has a sugar, base, and phosphate unit. **Deoxyribonucleic acid (DNA)** stores hereditary information in your cells while **ribonucleic acid (RNA)** is responsible for making proteins. Finally, a very important biological molecule that must be mentioned is **adenosine triphosphate (ATP)**, which provides the cell's fuel. It is similar to the structure of nucleic acids, but acts like carbohydrates and fat in its ability to store energy. However, the energy of an ATP molecule can be used immediately. Cells must have a steady supply of ATP in order to survive.

CELL STRUCTURE

All cells have a structure that consists of a cytoplasm, ribosomes, and an outer cell membrane. The structural components of eukaryotic cells of animals are described here.

Cytoplasm

The interior of the cell is the **cytoplasm**. In eukaryotic cells, the cytoplasm contains the various organelles that carry out the activities of the cell. The liquid part of the cytoplasm, called the cytosol, holds the various organelles. The cytosol was once thought of as a soup that the organelles float around in, but we now know this is not the case. Organelles are organized in a set arrangement and are not free-floating within the cytosol. Animals, including humans, have more organelles than plants.

Eukaryotic Cell

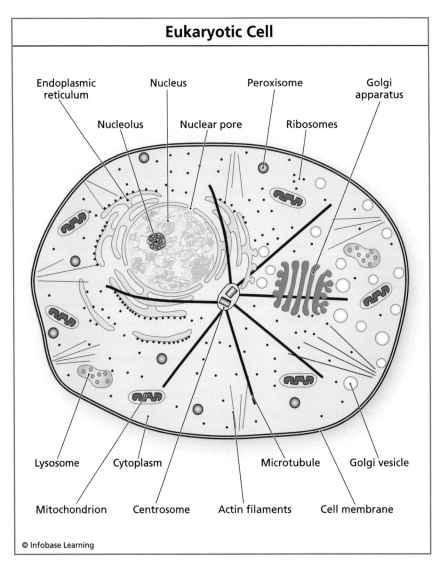

FIGURE 1.2 A eukaryotic cell contains membrane-bound compartments in which metabolic activities take place. The nucleus contains DNA; other organelles perform specific functions.

Organelles

Several cell structures that are found in the cytoplasm perform essential functions to maintain life. What follows is a description of the organelles of typical animal eukaryotic cells.

The **endoplasmic reticulum (ER)**, which is the largest of the internal membranes, is the cell's own circulatory system. The endoplasmic reticulum is a network of internal membranes that functions to form compartments and vesicles. This organelle also participates in protein and lipid synthesis. Specifically, **rough endoplasmic reticulum** makes proteins for export. The surface is studded with **ribosomes** that translate RNA copies of genes into protein. These proteins are either secreted outside the cells or are incorporated into membranes. **Smooth endoplasmic reticulum** has many embedded enzymes that are responsible for catalyzing the synthesis of lipids and carbohydrates. So, as expected, smooth ER is housed in cells that perform extensive lipid synthesis. These cells are found in the intestine, testes, and brain. Smooth ER enzymes located in the liver are responsible for the detoxification of drugs. Another important function of the smooth ER is the storage of calcium ions (charged atoms) that are necessary for muscle contraction. The same ribosome organelle found in the endoplasmic reticulum can also be found freely in the cytosol.

The **Golgi apparatus** works with the endoplasmic reticulum to collect, package, and deliver protein molecules. These flattened membrane sacs are individually called Golgi bodies. **Lysosomes**—vesicles formed

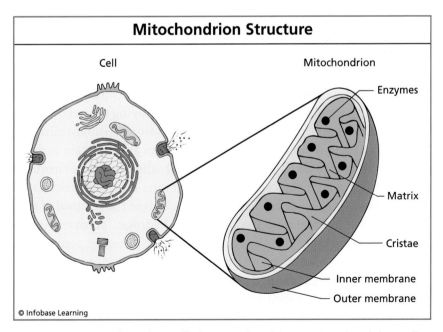

Mitochondrion Structure

Cell

Mitochondrion

Enzymes

Matrix

Cristae

Inner membrane

Outer membrane

© Infobase Learning

FIGURE 1.3 Located inside a cell, the mitochondrion is considered the "cell power plant" because it generates most of the cell's supply of adenosine triphosphate, which serves as a source of chemical energy.

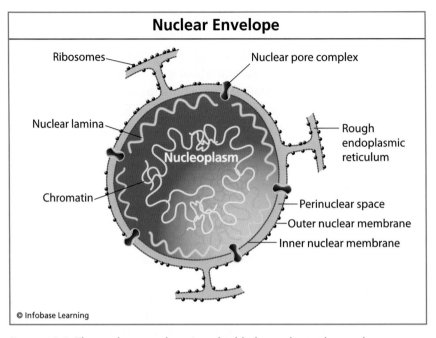

Nuclear Envelope

Ribosomes

Nuclear pore complex

Nuclear lamina

Rough endoplasmic reticulum

Nucleoplasm

Chromatin

Perinuclear space

Outer nuclear membrane

Inner nuclear membrane

© Infobase Learning

FIGURE 1.4 The nuclear envelope is a double-layered membrane that surrounds the contents of the nucleus. The nuclear pores consist of a complex of proteins that regulate the entry and exit of large particles.

from the Golgi apparatus—contain enzymes that digest worn-out organelles and wastes. These organelles function in a certain type of cell death known as **phagocytosis**. Lysosomes also destroy harmful bacteria and assist in human embryonic development by destroying the webbing cells between the fingers of a fetus. (However, lysosomal storage diseases, such as Tay-Sachs disease, can be fatal.) **Vacuoles** also function to digest byproducts, but are small or absent in animal cells. They store chemicals and maintain water balance. Another membrane-enclosed vesicle is the **peroxisome.** This vesicle has enzymes that catalyze the removal of electrons and hydrogen atoms. The byproduct, hydrogen peroxide, is created by the peroxisome, which is harmful to cells. However, peroxisomes contain the enzyme catalase, which breaks down the hydrogen peroxide.

The cell's powerhouse is the **mitochondria.** This organelle converts the chemical energy of food into the chemical energy of ATP. While the outer membrane of the mitochondria is smooth, the inner membrane contains highly-folded **cristae,** which contain enzymes that make ATP. (The inside of a mitochondria organelle looks almost like a woodlouse or pill bug flipped on its back with its legs pulled inward.) The mitochondrial matrix is the inner, fluid-filled compartment where many chemical reactions of cellular respiration occur. Mitochondria have their own DNA with genes that produce proteins used in oxidative metabolism. Interestingly, eukaryotic cells do not produce new mitochondria each time a cell divides. Instead, the mitochondria split in two when the cell divides and are distributed between the two new cells.

Nucleus

The information center of the cell is the **nucleus**, which is only found in eukaryotic cells. DNA located on several linear **chromosomes** inside the nucleus allows the cell to replicate. DNA and RNA synthesis occurs in the nucleus. Most eukaryotic cells have a single nucleus. The surface of the nucleus is enclosed by two phospholipid bilayer membranes called the **nuclear envelope.** Nuclear pores indent the surface of the nucleus and are filled with proteins. These proteins act as channels, allowing the passage of proteins and RNA/protein-RNA complexes. Within the nucleus, the **nucleolus** is the site where the individual subunits of ribosomes (rRNA and protein) are synthesized. These subunits move through the nuclear pores to the cytoplasm where they are assembled. Again, ribosomes are the sites of protein synthesis. A metabolically active organ such as the liver can contain millions of ribosomes. Another organelle located near the nucleus is the centrosome. Centrosomes that contain **centrioles** are observed in spindle formation during mitotic cell division, but their role is not entirely understood.

Other Organelles for Support and Movement

The protein-fiber **cytoskeleton** of a cell includes **cilia** and **flagella**. Among other activities, these cytoskeleton structures anchor organelles, move organelles within entire cells, and transmit signals from the exterior of the cell to the interior. In addition, cilia on cells located in the windpipe help remove dirt from the airway, while flagella propel sperm to the ova. Examples of other cytoskeleton structures include the extensions on the ends of a **neuron** (nerve cell). On one end, the **dendrites** receive signals; on the other end, **axons** transmit signals.

Cell Membrane

The cell's outer wall, which interacts with the surrounding environment, is called the **cell membrane** (also called the plasma membrane). However, it does so much more than just contain and protect the organelles of the interior cytoplasm.

The cell membrane takes in molecules from the surrounding environment, disposes of wastes, and performs chemical reactions. The cell membrane is **selectively permeable**, which means it allows some substances, such as oxygen and carbon dioxide, through a lipid bilayer, while it prevents other substances from getting in. Across the structure of the lipid bilayer of the cell membrane, there are protein passageways that allow substances and information to cross the membrane. These transmembrane proteins act as carriers, channels, and receptors. Transmembrane proteins within the cell membrane serve an important role as the sodium and potassium channels in nerve cells. Transmembrane proteins are also used in the transport of sugar, peptide hormones, and neurotransmitters. Among their many noteworthy activities, transmembrane proteins can act as enzymes—biological catalysts that increase the rate of a chemical reaction in the body.

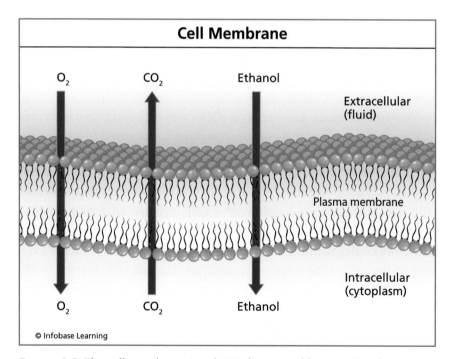

Cell Membrane

O_2 CO_2 Ethanol

Extracellular (fluid)

Plasma membrane

Intracellular (cytoplasm)

O_2 CO_2 Ethanol

© Infobase Learning

FIGURE 1.5 The cell membrane is selectively permeable, meaning that some substances can pass through it and some cannot. Fat-soluble substances, such as oxygen, carbon dioxide, and alcohol, pass through cell membranes by simple diffusion because they can dissolve in the lipid bilayer.

The interior protein network of the cell membrane can determine the shape of the cell, such as the red blood cell, or can anchor certain proteins to specific sites. Another important component of the cell membrane is the **cell surface marker**. The immune system's ability to recognize "safe" additions to the body, which is vital in organ transplants, happens in this component of the cell membrane. The body's recognition of the A, B, and O blood groups also occurs via cell surface markers.

MOVING MATERIALS INTO AND OUT OF CELLS

Passive Transport Works Without Expending Energy

Instead of using cellular energy to move a substance through a cell membrane, **passive transport** uses **diffusion** to move particles from an area of higher concentration to an area with lower concentration to create equilibrium. For example, oxygen diffuses into the bloodstream by this method. Other forms of passive transport include osmosis (the net water movement across a membrane by diffusion) and facilitated diffusion (in which selective protein channels called pores allow certain molecules through, but not others, because the plasma membrane is selectively permeable). Dialysis is yet another form of diffusion. In dialysis, a solution of crystalloids and colloids is separated from water by a membrane that is permeable only to the crystalloids. (This is the activity carried out for people undergoing kidney dialysis.)

Bulk Passage

While **exocytosis** is the process by which hormones, neurotransmitters, digestive enzymes, and other substances are secreted, **endocytosis** is the process by which cells absorb molecules by engulfing them. Eukaryotic cells perform a specific form of endocytosis called phagocytosis to ingest waste products, such as bacteria, dead tissue cells, and mineral particles. Phagocytosis is involved in the acquisition of nutrients for some cells, and it is a major mechanism used to remove disease-causing organisms and cell debris in the human immune system.

Another type of transport used by eukaryotic cells is receptor-mediated endocytosis. Low-density lipoproteins (LDL cholesterol) are an example of a molecule taken up by receptor-mediated endocytosis. These are the so-called "bad" cholesterol molecules that bring cholesterol into the cell where it can be incorporated into membranes. In

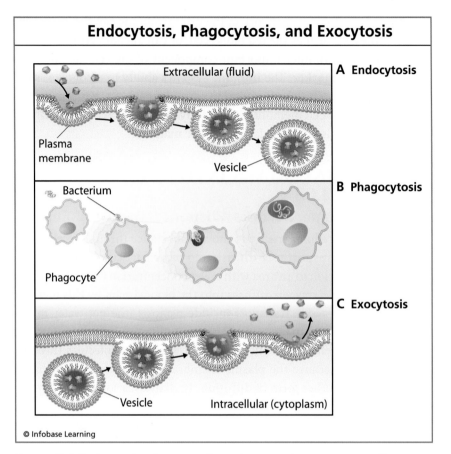

Endocytosis, Phagocytosis, and Exocytosis

Extracellular (fluid)

A Endocytosis

Plasma membrane

Vesicle

B Phagocytosis

Bacterium

Phagocyte

C Exocytosis

Vesicle   Intracellular (cytoplasm)

© Infobase Learning

FIGURE 1.6 Endocytosis, phagocytosis, and exocytosis are processes for moving substances into and out of cells. In endocytosis and phagocytosis, the cell membrane surrounds the particles and closes around them, drawing the particles into the cell. Phagocytosis is used primarily by white blood cells to engulf and destroy bacteria, viruses, and other large, foreign particles that could harm the body. Exocytosis is the reverse of endocytosis. The particles, contained within a vesicle, move to the edge of the cell, where the vesicle fuses with the cell membrane and releases the particles to the outside of the cell.

hypercholesteremia, for example, cholesterol stays in the bloodstream where it forms arterial plaques.

Active Transport Processes

Cells must expend energy to allow **active transport** of molecules across a membrane. Unlike passive transport, active transport allows the movement of molecules against the concentration gradient. A good example of this is the transport of sugar into liver cells where the concentration gradient is already higher than the surrounding blood plasma.

Active transport occurs when a transport protein binds to the solute and then a second binding site grabs the phosphate group from the ATP. The surge of energy from this reaction triggers a release of the original solute molecule. A second solute molecule from the side where the first molecule was released is picked up. After the release of the ATP phosphate group, the second molecule is released to the other side (the original side of the first solute molecule).

Active transport systems are involved in important biological processes including the sodium-potassium (Na-K+) pump. (This process helps nerve cells generate signals.) Another example is the glucose transport carrier.

WHAT MAKES HUMAN CELLS "HUMAN"?

Humans tend to view themselves as different from and superior to other animals in the animal kingdom. Numerous traits show that humans are unique among other creatures. In fact, the human practice of classification is one example of such a characteristic. A high level of intelligence allows humans to use language, reasoning, and tools. We have emotions and empathy for other humans and creatures. We have opposable thumbs and walk upright. Humans even have the ability to create the concept of time. However, because we are human, our scientific experiments have revealed that several other species have many of these abilities, too. For example, elephants show empathy and grief when a fellow elephant dies. Chimpanzees' use of language has been shown in laboratory experiments, but whales and dolphins also communicate with each other. Chimps and otters both use tools in the wild.

If this is all true, what is it then that truly makes humans unique? Perhaps a view at the cellular level can provide some clues that will help answer this question. Humans are comprised of eukaryotic cells, as all animals are. Scientific discovery has supported Charles Darwin's theory of evolution. *Homo sapiens*, individual creatures of the human lineage, are believed to have existed for only the last 250,000 years, but recent scientific discoveries may alter this finding. (A generational comparison of DNA shows a common ancestor among humans may have been much more recent—only 6,500 years.) Recent research shows that humans are genetically highly *homologous*, which means we are more alike among ourselves than other species. Still, we exhibit a good deal of genetic diversity. Humans are still evolving, according to some researchers, who point out the lengthening of the reproductive cycle as well as the reductions in cholesterol, blood glucose, and blood pressure among humans. (Although these levels can be altered by the conscious efforts of humans, the ability to physiologically change the amounts of cholesterol, blood glucose, and blood pressure shows a genetic ability for self-modification.)

It is commonly accepted that there is a 98.5% similarity between the DNA of chimpanzees and humans. This is based on a study of more than 19.8 million bases in humans and chimpanzees. However, even this incredible number of genetic bases only represents less than 1% of the human genome—the complete set of genes that make up human genetic material.

Genetic differences are not the only unique aspect between human and animal cells. Among the trillions of cells in the human body, there are about 200 cell types that exhibit great variation in their size, shape, and function. The varying sizes of cells, from the smallest sperm cell to the longest motor neuron in the leg, already have been mentioned. We only need a microscope to see that a sperm cell has a different shape than a skin cell. Human cells are highly specialized for their particular function. The cells of the eye absorb light and then convert it to electrical energy to be interpreted by the brain. Only muscle cells have myofilaments, which allow the cells to contract and produce movement.

The human blood cell also shows interesting characteristics, some of which are shared with animals. We find blood typing of A, B, O, and AB as well as the **Rh (rhesus) factors** on red blood cells in both humans and animals. Only mammalian animals, humans included, lose the nuclei of the red blood cells in order to carry more oxygen. Unlike certain animals, human blood cells carry all five types of leukocytes (white blood cells): neutrophils, eosinophils, basophils, lymphocytes, and monocytes. The adhesive quality of platelets also varies among animals, including humans.

However, these functions are shared with animals. In that case, what other unique differences of human cells can we find? As it turns out, glycobiology, the study of sugars in biology, has recently uncovered another one-of-a-kind characteristic of human cells. The most common kind of polysaccharide that covers the human cell surface is a type of sialic acid called N-acetyl neuraminic acid, or Neu5Ac. Humans are the only animal that has this molecule, which only differs by one oxygen molecule from the sialic acid on the cell surface of other animals. What advantage did this mutation provide humans? Although we do not know the answer to this question, we do know that a certain form of malaria that adheres to the cell surface in animals is not found in humans. However, we see other forms of malaria in humans. In fact, human-specific illnesses are another unique feature of being human. We are the only animals to have asthma and Parkinson's disease, among other illnesses. We continue to learn the specific characteristics that make human cells "human."

WHY ARE CELLS IMPORTANT TO HUMAN HEALTH?

Homeostasis is the balance of proper activity in a cell, and it is crucial to continued good health. Cells also comprise the food we eat, which is the

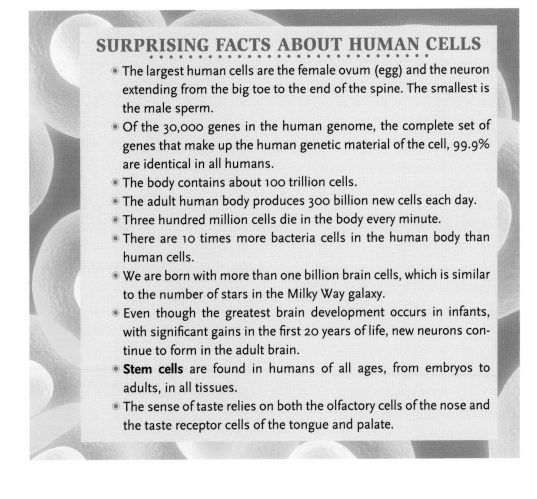

SURPRISING FACTS ABOUT HUMAN CELLS

- The largest human cells are the female ovum (egg) and the neuron extending from the big toe to the end of the spine. The smallest is the male sperm.
- Of the 30,000 genes in the human genome, the complete set of genes that make up the human genetic material of the cell, 99.9% are identical in all humans.
- The body contains about 100 trillion cells.
- The adult human body produces 300 billion new cells each day.
- Three hundred million cells die in the body every minute.
- There are 10 times more bacteria cells in the human body than human cells.
- We are born with more than one billion brain cells, which is similar to the number of stars in the Milky Way galaxy.
- Even though the greatest brain development occurs in infants, with significant gains in the first 20 years of life, new neurons continue to form in the adult brain.
- **Stem cells** are found in humans of all ages, from embryos to adults, in all tissues.
- The sense of taste relies on both the olfactory cells of the nose and the taste receptor cells of the tongue and palate.

energy source for our cells. Certain cells, such as those of certain bacteria, make us sick, while cells of other kinds of bacteria can help us maintain good health. Many different types of cells work together in organs that comprise the organ systems of our bodies, including blood cells, neurons, epithelial cells, gland cells, and ova and sperm of the reproductive system.

Cellular activity is carried out in a specific manner. If certain components or activities of the cell are missing, the cell does not function properly, resulting in imbalances we regard as illnesses. Cells are the basic unit of all life, including humans. Without cells, we would not exist. Therefore, it is important to understand how we can keep our cells healthy and what new discoveries are being made about the awesome human cell.

2

Cytology: The History of Cell Study and Its Effects on Human Health

THE MICROSCOPE REVEALS THE SMALLEST ENTITIES

The incredible knowledge we have of cells today would not have been possible without the earlier inventions in optics and the creation of optical lenses. While there is a debate about who should receive credit for the first microscope, the invention is usually attributed to lens makers Hans Lippershey and Zacharias Janssen who each made their own microscope in the year 1595. Early versions included both the simple microscope (a long tube and a single lens) and the compound microscope (with multiple lenses). Galileo Galilei improved upon the compound microscope in 1625 with a focusing device.

Shortly thereafter, researchers used the microscope to study anatomy and cells. In Italy in the 1640s, an ordained priest and self-taught scientist, Giambattista Odierna, studied the eyes of flies and the poison glands of vipers through a microscope. In 1661, the first published research of Italian physician Marcello Malpighi described how he used the microscope to study the lung, skin, liver, and kidney. His work has led others to call him the founder of microscopic anatomy. Malpighi's studies advanced the science of embryology and furthered what was known about blood and skin

FIGURE 2.1 Because of his studies involving the human body, Italian physician Marcello Malpighi has had many microscopic anatomical structures named after him, including a skin layer (actually the unit of the stratum basale and the stratum spinosum) and two Malpighian corpuscles in the kidneys and the spleen.

at that time. (He may also have been the first to see red blood cells under a microscope.)

In England in 1665, scientist Robert Hooke recorded his microscopic observations of the cell in an impressive book titled *Micrographia* that contained detailed illustrations of living organisms. In this book, Hooke also first coined the term *cell* for the smallest part of a plant as way of describing the small pores he observed in a thin sample of cork. (Actually, what he saw were cell walls; there were no internal structures of the cell, such as the nucleus or organelles). He chose the word *cell* because the pores reminded him of the cells lived in by Catholic monks.

Even though it is possible that Malpighi was the first to see blood cells, the discovery of those particular cells has been attributed to Antonie van Leeuwenhoek, of the Netherlands, who was also the first to identify spermatozoa. In 1674, he observed the algae *Spirogyra* and called the moving organisms "animalcules." It is also believed that he was the first to observe bacteria. In 1676, van Leeuwenhoek was the first to report the existence of microorganisms.

Microscopy was improved upon with the development of light microscopes, which could illuminate samples and greatly enhance the ability to view a cell's small structures. However, the invention of the first electron microscope in 1933 by German physicist Ernst Ruska truly changed the way microscopic images were generated. Instead of slicing specimens, scientists now painted them with a thin layer of metal. Another advancement was made in 1986, when Heinrich Rohrer and Gerd Binnig created the scanning tunneling microscope that provides three-dimensional atomic scale images on metal or semiconductor surfaces. Around the same time, the digital microscope, equipped with a digital camera, was developed to allow observation via a computer. To perform specific tasks, other optical microscope versions have been developed, including the stereo microscope (with stereoscopic view), comparison microscope (to compare two samples in one image), inverted microscope (to study samples from below), and the student microscope (a low-cost, durable version for schools).

UNDERSTANDING DISEASE AND HEREDITY: THE CONTRIBUTIONS OF CELL AND GERM THEORIES

Today, most of us understand that life is generated from life, and we have a basic knowledge of how our body functions. We know that certain organs and their cells are responsible for different bodily functions, such as breathing, digestion, and circulation. We also understand that good health is, in part, the result of practicing good hygiene, eating healthy, and exercising. However, this knowledge, which may be quite simple, is quite an advancement over what our ancestors knew.

Before the discovery of cells, scientists looked for ways to explain where diseases came from. Famous Greek philosophers Plato and Aristotle, and even the "Father of Medicine," Hippocrates, who was considered the greatest physician of his time, believed that the body contained four "humors" (called choleric, sanguine, phlegmatic, and melancholy), that controlled health, disease, and bodily functions. Health was seen as the balance of humors with blood as the source of life. (This idea of humors actually was considered an advancement in Hippocrates's era when people believed illness was due to evil spirits.) The belief that these humors caused illness continued into the Renaissance and Elizabethan times. Sanguine humor was represented by blood, choleric humor by yellow bile, phlegmatic humor by phlegm, and melancholic humor by black bile. The humors were also associated with various earth elements, complexions, and personality traits. Similar ideas were held by Chinese and Islamic medicine.

The humors represent a theory known as vitalism, in which each organism is distinct with an energy or soul that is not represented in biochemical reactions. The theory also states that science is not the sole determinant of health, but rather that the life of an individual is also partly self-determined. New Age philosophies and some religions, including Christian Science, appear to incorporate some of this ideology. Conversely, scientific theory only supports what is proven with scientific experimentation.

Another concept that was popular at the time was spontaneous generation, which supported the idea that life could arise from nonliving matter. An example that seemed to support this idea was the sudden appearance of maggots in rotting meat (a mistake that early observers made when they failed to notice the presence of fly larvae).

Vitalism was replaced by objective scientific experimentation and the support of various theories, including cell theory. The idea that all plants and animals are made of cells has been credited to German botanist Matthias Schleiden in 1838 and zoologist Theodor Schwann in 1839. However, it is suggested that Czech scientist Jan Evangelista Purkyně observed "granules" of plants under the microscope in 1835 before the cell theory was developed. In 1855, German scientist Rudolf Virchow proposed that all cells come from the division of cells that already exist (although many believe this idea should be credited to fellow scientist Robert Remak). These ideas about the cellular composition of all organisms and the process of cell reproduction resulting in daughter cells make up the cell theory.

The **germ theory** has been credited to van Leeuwenhoek for his discovery of microorganisms. Germ theory states that disease is caused by microorganisms that invade the body. (However, others may have had these same ideas much, much earlier than van Leeuwenhoek, even before the invention of the microscope.) The idea of germ theory was further supported by French scientist Louis Pasteur who said the biogenesis (creation of life) of bacteria in milk and meat caused diseases. (The process he used to kill these organisms, which increased food safety tremendously, is known as **pasteurization**.) Pasteur extended this idea of disease-causing microorganisms to humans, which later gave rise to the use of **antiseptic** techniques during surgery by Joseph Lister in 1867. These theories refuted the ideas of spontaneous generation and humors. In 1876, German physician Robert Koch identified a specific bacterium, which is now known as *Bacillus anthracis*, in the blood of cows with anthrax. (This bacterium has been in the news in the last decade as a potential biological terrorism agent.) From this discovery, Koch's postulates were developed to determine whether particular bacteria were the cause of specific diseases. These postulates are as follows:

1. The same pathogen (disease-causing organism) must be identified in each animal with a disease.
2. The pathogen must be isolated (taken) from the host animal, and grown in a culture without any other cells.
3. The pathogen grown in culture must be injected into a healthy animal that then gets the disease.
4. The same pathogen is isolated and identified from the experimental animals that were injected with the pathogen of the grown culture.

From Koch's postulates, microbiologists can now identify bacteria, viruses, protists, fungi, and parasitic worms. People today have a more scientific view of how our cells and organ systems function.

THE HISTORY OF VARIOLATION AND INOCULATION

Interestingly, although the scientific study of germs would not begin until the 1800s, the concept of imparting immunity to people through the use of body fluids already infected with disease occurred hundreds of years beforehand. There is evidence that practitioners of both Chinese medicine in the second century A.D. and of Indian medicine in the eighth century A.D. collected the fluid and scabs of people with the smallpox virus and

FIGURE 2.2 German physician Robert Koch was awarded the Nobel Prize in physiology or medicine in 1905 for his tuberculosis studies. Because of his research, he is considered the father of clinical microbiology.

gave it to otherwise healthy people to give them immunity to smallpox (also known as variola).

This practice of **inoculation** was introduced in England in 1721 by the wife of the British ambassador to the Ottoman Empire, Lady Mary Wortley Montagu, who witnessed "variolations" performed while she was in Constantinople. The idea became very popular given the high mortality rate of smallpox at the time. In the 1700s, an estimated 60 million Europeans died of smallpox. The death rate varied by country and time period, ranging from 20% to 60%. Babies fared even worse, with 80% of infants in London and 98% of babies in Berlin dying of the disease in the late 1800s. The effectiveness of inoculation was readily noted, but skeptics were concerned about getting the disease from the **vaccination**.

Certainly, there was risk in using variolation, and direct contact with body fluids of smallpox victims was quite dangerous. Early on in the Far East, practitioners had discovered that scabs from the inside of noses of smallpox victims were less potent. Edward Jenner built on this idea of safer inoculation and developed the first vaccine for smallpox from the animal version, cowpox, in 1796. (However, some contest that this discovery was actually made by Benjamin Jesty and others in 1774.) Jenner discovered that milk maids were less likely to contract smallpox, and developed a vaccination from the less-deadly strain of the disease. Jenner inoculated a young boy with the contents of cowpox blisters from a milkmaid's hand, and then injected the boy with smallpox. He found, remarkably, that the boy vaccinated with the similar cowpox was now immune to the disease. Because of this experiment, Britain began offering free cowpox vaccinations to people and outlawed the use of smallpox itself for vaccination.

Another 50 years or so would pass before Pasteur refined Jenner's technique of inoculation when he discovered that even older, weaker versions of bacterial cultures would still produce immunity in an inoculated individual. (Pasteur used chickens in his experiment.) However, a truer understanding of how immunity is imparted through exposure to disease wouldn't be known until the twentieth century.

Interestingly, scientists today still use fragments of cowpox virus to produce vaccinations for herpes simplex (chickenpox) and hepatitis. Until worldwide inoculation completely eliminated the disease, 60% of the world's population was still threatened by smallpox well into the twentieth century. According to the World Health Organization, the last naturally occurring case was in 1977 in Somalia and the last laboratory-derived case was in the United Kingdom in 1978.

A HISTORY OF THE UNDERSTANDING OF HOW CELLS ARISE

According to cell theory, cells are formed from other cells that already exist. The understanding we have about how this occurs is attributed to German biologist August Weismann in 1880. He reported that all of the cells that are alive today can be traced back to ancient times. Weismann's germ plasm theory, which refers to germ cells in general rather than disease-causing germs, states that the genetic material of cells comes from only the sex gametes, meaning the ova and sperm, of a parent cell and not the other (somatic) cells of the parents' bodies.

Around the same time, several other scientists made notable discoveries about cells, although some of these ideas actually overlap each other. Botanist Eduard Strasburger came up with the terms *nucleus* and *cytoplasm*. In 1876, Strasburger stated that new nuclei arise from the division of other cell nuclei (the process known as mitosis) in plants. In 1878, German biologist Walther Flemming identified mitosis in salamander fins. Flemming also reported on the existence of **chromatin**, the thread-like genetic material found in cell nuclei. Flemming was unaware of the work of Gregor Mendel in 1866, who experimented with pea plants to observe seven observable traits in plant offspring. Meiosis was first described in a sea urchin by Oscar Hertwig in 1876, and the process of how chromosomes combine at meiosis during gamete (sex cell) production, was described by Belgian Edouard van Beneden in 1883. Heinrich von Waldeyer-Hartz was the first to identify the neuron, and also coined the term *chromosomes*.

Yet the path to understanding cytology (the study of cells) was not effortless. These scientists did not all agree with each other's findings. For example, Virchow would not extend his observations about cell division to embrace Darwin's theory of evolution that was put forth during his lifetime. Also, Virchow also didn't believe bacteria caused illnesses.

And even though many of these observations about cells were made around the same time, it did not automatically result in theories about cell reproduction that were widely accepted. In 1890, the necessary role of meiosis in reproduction and inheritance was finally made by Weismann. He stated that two cell divisions were necessary to transform one **diploid** cell (a somatic or body cell) into four **haploid** cells (usually gametes or sex cells) if the number of chromosomes were to be maintained.

It wasn't until 1900 that Mendel's research on pea plants was rediscovered and found to have merit. Mendel's studies of pea plants further explained the role of genetics on cell reproduction as set forth by cell theory. From observations of traits that occurred more frequently, Mendel hypothesized the law of dominance. Although his original terms were changed, he put forth the ideas of **genes**, **alleles** (forms of genes for a trait), genotype (a combination of alleles), and **phenotype** (the physical or visible trait which each genotype determines).

THE INTRODUCTION OF ANTIBIOTICS

Just like Pasteur, who made his discoveries when he left a culture sitting out too long, the Scottish biologist Sir Alexander Fleming made an error that led to the discovery of both lysozymes and penicillin. Fleming had returned from a long vacation to find that one of his cultures had been contaminated with a fungus that had destroyed his colonies of staphylococci bacteria. The lysozymes had eliminated the bacteria, and the mold

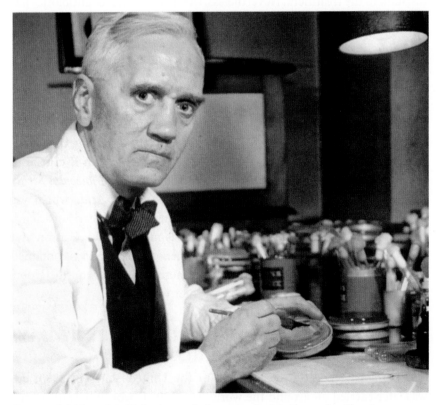

FIGURE 2.3 Scottish biologist and pharmacologist Alexander Fleming discovered penicillin from the mold *Penicillium notatum* in 1928.

that produced the lysozymes was from the *Penicillium* genus. (The mold juice was named *penicillin*.)

This significant discovery, made in 1928, eventually changed the practice of medicine. Before, antiseptic techniques mostly worked only on bacteria on the surface and not deep in wounds, such as those suffered by war veterans. Not only did penicillin work against staphylococci, but it also worked on pathogens that caused diseases such as pneumonia, meningitis, diphtheria, and scarlet fever. However, the first attempts to treat disease in humans were discouraging because penicillin worked slowly. It wasn't until 1940 when other scientists were able to produce an effective form of penicillin. By 1945, this new treatment entered mass production.

Unfortunately, the wonderful discovery of antibiotics was also deterred by another early discovery by Fleming—the existence of antibiotic resistance. Therefore, very early on, it was known that antibiotics should not be given unless the diagnosis supported it, because bacteria would become resistant to the treatment. Nevertheless, the introduction of antibiotics has saved millions of lives globally.

WATSON AND CRICK: FURTHERING KNOWLEDGE ABOUT DNA

In 1953, James D. Watson and Francis Crick proposed the idea of a double helix structure of the DNA molecule based on the research of other scientists. They also developed the Watson-Crick base pairing of nucleotides (guanine to cytosine and adenine to thymine), which is crucial to the understanding of genetic instructions. Their article, *"Molecular Structure of Nucleic Acids: A Structure for Deoxyribose Nucleic Acid,"* which was published in the scientific journal *Nature,* is known as a "pearl" of science because although it is brief, its importance is monumental. Watson and Crick's ideas explained the mystery of how genetic instructions contained in cells were passed from generation to generation. They won the Nobel Prize with Maurice Wilkins in 1962 for their work.

UNDERSTANDING HUMAN GENETICS TODAY: THE HUMAN GENOME PROJECT

The Human Genome Project began in the United States in 1990, but was later carried on around the world. In 2000, a "working draft" of the genome was announced, with information about the sequence of the last genome published in 2006. The goal of the Human Genome Project is to understand the genetic makeup of the human species, but it has also produced information about other living organisms. The original idea was to map the three billion chemical units in the human genetic set, but the project would have been too costly. Thus, researchers concentrated on mapping only the sites on the genome where the likelihood of variations is the greatest.

The project involved sequencing the multiple variations of each gene. Although researchers mapped the human haploid reference genome, they still have not sequenced about 8% of the total genome. Researchers with the Human Genome Project also have not yet mapped the diploid human genome, which is the most common cell of the body. The Human Genome Project is important because knowledge about the unique DNA among individuals can revolutionize the diagnosis, treatment, and prevention of diseases. Work on the project has led to the following discoveries about human biology:

- There are 20,500 genes in humans.
- Only 1.1% to 1.4% of the genome's sequence codes for proteins.
- There are more segmental duplications (repeated sections of DNA) in humans than in other mammals.
- When the research about the Human Genome Project was published, it was believed that less than 7% of the protein families mapped were specific to vertebrate species.

AIDS, EBOLA, AND HEPATITIS C: IDENTIFYING NEW DISEASES

Discoveries in the field of cytology continue. Every year, scientists identify new organisms, both plant and animal. Not all of these discoveries have been for the better though. In 1981, **acquired immunodeficiency syndrome (AIDS)** was named, which is the disease expression of **human immunodeficiency virus (HIV)**. In humans, the disease destroys the immune system's ability to fight infection. The virus is related to the simian immunodeficiency virus (SIV) that infects apes and monkeys in Africa, with the earliest infection of HIV-1 documented in the Congo in 1959. However, genetic studies indicate that the very first case of human infection may even have occurred as early as 1910. Another deadly virus that emerged in the Congo was the Ebola virus, with the first known case around 1976. This virus causes uncontrolled bleeding in the body. Also, in the 1970s, the hepatitis C virus was identified, which only causes disease

PEOPLE WHO STUDY CELLS AND HUMAN HEALTH

There are many types of scientists who study cells and human health. Here are some of them:

- *Cytologists* study changes in cellular composition with a microscope.
- *Histologists* study histological tissues, including epithelial tissue, muscular tissue, connective tissue, and nervous tissue.
- *Medical technologists* analyze samples from humans with tests in chemistry, genetics, hematology, immunology, microbiology, serology, urinalysis, and body fluid analysis to diagnose and treat human illnesses.
- *Microbial geneticists* study the hereditary characteristics of microorganisms.
- *Microbial physiologists* study microbial function and biology
- *Microbiologists* study microbes (single-celled organisms). These include the following occupations:
  - *Bacteriologists* study bacteria.
  - *Environmental microbiologists* study the microorganisms in the environment.
  - *Food microbiologists* work in the food industry where they study food-borne illnesses and spoilage.
  - *Immunologists* study how the body defends itself.
  - *Industrial microbiologists* work in biotechnology to create useful medical products.
  - *Medical microbiologists* are physicians who specialize in the diagnosis of disease.
  - *Microbial epidemiologists* study the role of microorganisms in illnesses.
  - *Mycologists* study fungi.
  - *Protozoologists* study protists.
  - *Virologists* study viruses.
- *Pathologists* study and diagnose diseases; the field of pathology includes various subspecialties, such as clinical pathology, which uses laboratory analysis of body fluids to diagnose disease.

in humans. To date, there are no vaccinations for HIV, Ebola, or hepatitis C. However, experimental vaccines are currently being studied. In May 2010, an experimental vaccine for Ebola was introduced that appeared to produce **antibodies** to several species of the disease. Even though there have been advancements in vaccinations for certain viral infections like herpes simplex (chickenpox and shingles), other infections, including the short-lived, yet pesky, cold virus, continue to elude effective treatment (though their symptoms are treatable). If there has been anything positive about the discovery of such viruses, it is that the study of them has furthered our understanding of cells.

ADVANCES IN CYTOLOGY RESEARCH

Through cellular biology, scientists continue to identify diseases as well as their prevention and treatment. Recent advances have included a vaccination for cervical cancer and treatments for other cancers. To combat influenza each year, the Centers for Disease Control (CDC) and the World Health Organization (WHO) identify the most virulent strains of influenza and help guide the production of effective vaccinations, including the swine flu (H1N1), avian bird flu (H5N1A), and others. These groups need to be on the alert for changes in influenza strains because they mutate rapidly. Similarly, it is hoped that pharmaceutical companies will decide to return to antibiotic research given the surge in antibiotic-resistant strains of bacteria, including *Staphylococcus aureus* and *Clostridium difficile.*

3

How Cells
Work Together

HOW DO HUMAN CELLS ORIGINATE?

There are many ideas about how life originated on Earth. There is the creationist theory of a higher power, the idea that life originated on other planets and came here, and the theory that life spontaneously originated and evolved from a cesspool of chemicals that could support it. Science may not have answered the question about where life began so far, but we do know a lot about the biological background of humans. There is scientific evidence that supports Charles Darwin's theory of evolution as well as the theory that all humans are related to a common ancestor (though there is even some debate among scientists about the common ancestry theory).

So how do cells come together to form a new human being? Cellular biology explains how gametes (sex cells) combine to produce new life, multiply exponentially, and also differentiate to become a unique human being. To explain how all this occurs, an understanding of the processes of mitosis and meiosis is needed.

Most of the cells in the human body are called **somatic cells** and are produced through the process of division known as mitosis. However, the ova and sperm are gametes, or sex cells. These are also known as haploid cells, which means they have half of the chromosomes of the parent cell. There are considerably fewer haploid cells than diploid cells (each of which has 46 chromosomes) in the human body. (In fact, the gametes and a few other specialized cells are the only haploid cells in the body.)

When a haploid sperm cell fertilizes a haploid ova cell, the nuclei of the egg and sperm fuse. This results in the formation of a **zygote,** a diploid cell that continues to divide via mitosis. This single cell becomes the human fetus, and gives rise to all of the other cells in the human body. In the zygote, only a few cells are set aside early in development to become sex cells. Although these are diploid cells as well, the gamete-producing, germ-line cells undergo meiosis rather than mitosis. (An explanation of meiosis will be given after an explanation of mitosis.)

Because the biology of the egg is so complex, it only allows for **fertilization** by the same species via species-specific protein molecules and receptor proteins. Also, once the ovum is fertilized, a barrier is quickly formed to prevent further fertilization by additional sperm. This prevents the nucleus from containing too many chromosomes. However, this does not prevent the creation of twins by a fertilized egg that divides (creating identical twins) or the fertilization of two eggs by two sperm at the same time (creating fraternal twins). (The creation of triplets, quadruplets, and more also follow this pattern of more than one egg being fertilized by additional sperm. However, identical twins can also be included in with triplets, quadruplets, and more.)

Newborn babies are not delivered with all of the cells that they will need for the rest of their lives. Even at birth, the process of cell division is not complete, and the cells in a newborn baby's body do not simply grow in size. Instead, throughout a human lifespan, including the period of time in the mother's womb (gestation), cells are continually dividing, living, and dying. The majority of cell growth is complete between the ages of 18 and 21 years. There are only a few notable exceptions to this, including nerve, skeletal muscle, and red blood cells; these cells do not divide once they mature. Largely through the process of mitosis, the adult human body produces 300 billion new cells each day, and 300 million cells die in the body every minute.

THE CELL CYCLE AND MITOSIS CELL DIVISION

A cell usually passes through the stages of mitosis cell division within 8 to 20 hours. Before a cell enters the stages of mitosis, it spends most of its time in **interphase,** a period during which no cell division occurs. Normal life activities occur during this stage. Chromosomes are also duplicated

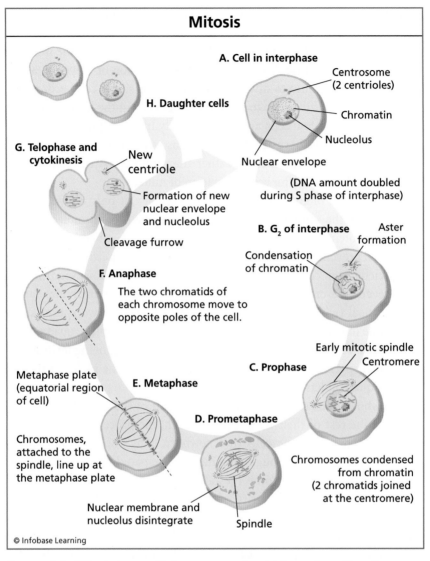

Mitosis

A. Cell in interphase

Centrosome
(2 centrioles)

H. Daughter cells

Chromatin

Nucleolus

G. Telophase and cytokinesis

New centriole

Nuclear envelope

Formation of new nuclear envelope and nucleolus

(DNA amount doubled during S phase of interphase)

Cleavage furrow

B. G₂ of interphase

Aster formation

Condensation of chromatin

F. Anaphase

The two chromatids of each chromosome move to opposite poles of the cell.

Metaphase plate (equatorial region of cell)

E. Metaphase

Early mitotic spindle

Centromere

C. Prophase

D. Prometaphase

Chromosomes, attached to the spindle, line up at the metaphase plate

Chromosomes condensed from chromatin (2 chromatids joined at the centromere)

Nuclear membrane and nucleolus disintegrate

Spindle

© Infobase Learning

FIGURE 3.1 Mitosis is a multistage process in which a eukaryotic cell separates the chromosomes in its cell nucleus into two identical sets of nuclei.

during this stage to create a pair of sister **chromatids** that contain identical, double-stranded DNA sequences. The phases of interphase are known as the G_1 phase, then the S phase, and finally, the G_2 phase.

Biologists typically consider mitosis as occurring in the following stages: prophase, metaphase, anaphase, and telophase. In early **prophase**, the nuclear envelope and then the nucleolus disappear. Long chromatin fibers begin to condense and become visible chromosomes. During late prophase, prometaphase, chromosomes continue to thicken and condense. The centrioles migrate to the poles of the cell and, from there, spindles form between the centrioles. Each chromosome consists of a pair of sister chromatids, each of which has a constricted region called a **centromere**.

In the next phase, **metaphase**, spindle fibers attach to these kineto-chores that are lined up along the middle of the cell. During **anaphase**, chromatids separate at the centromeres, with one group of chromosomes migrating toward each pole. In the next phase, **telophase**, the chromosomes are at their respective poles, and, at that point, two nuclei form. During telophase, **cytokinesis** produces two daughter cells. A nuclear envelope for each of the two cells starts to develop. Finally, the cells enter interphase once more with daughter cells that are identical to the parent cell.

MEIOSIS CELL DIVISION FOR GAMETES

Unlike most of the other cells in the body, sex cells (or gametes, which were originally diploid cells) undergo meiosis in the reproductive organs of males and females to create haploid cells. A haploid cell from one human joins the haploid cell from another human when fertilized to become a diploid cell zygote.

The process of meiosis is distinctly different from mitosis because it results in haploid cells with half the number of chromosomes (n), 23, instead of diploid cells that each contain a full set of 46 chromosomes. The process reduces the chromosome number from diploid to haploid. There are two consecutive divisions, known as meiosis I and meiosis II, that result in the creation of four daughter cells. Before this division occurs, only one duplication of chromosomes occurs. Two centrosomes are located outside the nucleus, and each centrosome contains a pair of centrioles. The centrioles are produced by the duplication of a single centrosome during interphase before meiosis begins.

Meiosis I: Reduction Division

At the beginning of this stage, the cell enters prophase I. This is considered the most complex phase of the process and the cell spends about 90% of its time in this state. As in mitosis, the nuclear envelope breaks down. After the chromosomes are duplicated, homologous chromosomes (known as homologues), which are chromosomes that are similar in shape, size, and the genes that they carry, line up and pair closely with each other.

These pairs of homologues move to the center of the cell with the help of spindle fibers during metaphase I. In anaphase I, the homologues begin to separate with the help of the spindle fibers that pull them toward the opposite poles. The chromosome retains both chromatids joined by a

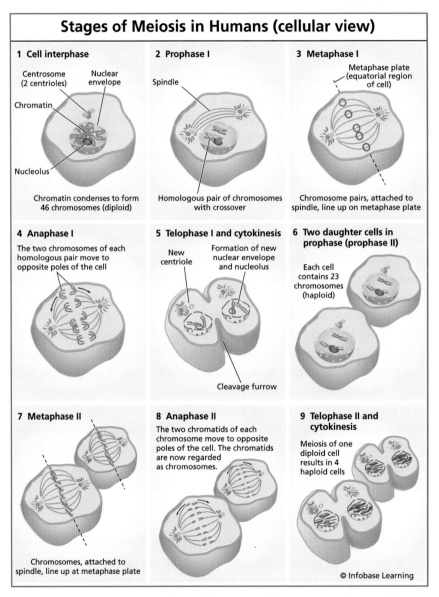

Stages of Meiosis in Humans (cellular view)

1 Cell interphase

Centrosome (2 centrioles)
Nuclear envelope
Chromatin
Nucleolus

Chromatin condenses to form 46 chromosomes (diploid)

2 Prophase I

Spindle

Homologous pair of chromosomes with crossover

3 Metaphase I

Metaphase plate (equatorial region of cell)

Chromosome pairs, attached to spindle, line up on metaphase plate

4 Anaphase I

The two chromosomes of each homologous pair move to opposite poles of the cell

5 Telophase I and cytokinesis

New centriole
Formation of new nuclear envelope and nucleolus

Cleavage furrow

6 Two daughter cells in prophase (prophase II)

Each cell contains 23 chromosomes (haploid)

7 Metaphase II

Chromosomes, attached to spindle, line up at metaphase plate

8 Anaphase II

The two chromatids of each chromosome move to opposite poles of the cell. The chromatids are now regarded as chromosomes.

9 Telophase II and cytokinesis

Meiosis of one diploid cell results in 4 haploid cells

© Infobase Learning

FIGURE 3.2 Meiosis in animals produces gametes (sperm and egg cells), necessary for sexual reproduction.

centromere. (This is unlike anaphase in mitosis, since the chromatids do *not* separate at their centromeres.)

During telophase I, the individual chromosomes gather at each pole and the cytoplasm divides, resulting in two cells (cytokinesis). Each cell produced contains half the number of chromosomes as the parent cell.

Meiosis II: Separation of Chromatids

Each of the two daughter cells created during meiosis I enters the stage of meiosis II, where sister chromatids separate. The process is similar to mitosis, but the initial cell is haploid as a result of meiosis I.

The first phase of meiosis II is prophase II, during which the chromosomes condense again and the nuclear envelope breaks down, but the DNA does not replicate again. A new spindle is formed and chromosomes move to the middle of the cell. In metaphase II, the spindle fibers bind to the centromeres and the kinetochores of sister chromatids of each chromosome point toward opposite poles. When the spindle fibers contract in anaphase II, the centromeres split and the sister chromatids move to opposite poles. Finally, in telophase II, nuclei form at the cell poles, and cytokinesis occurs. The nuclear envelope forms around the four sets of haploid daughter chromosomes.

CELL DIFFERENTIATION AND EMBRYONIC DEVELOPMENT

When a vertebrate zygote is formed, the rapid division that follows is called cleavage, and produces a ball of cells known as a blastula, which has a hollow, fluid-filled center called a blastocoel. Cleavage is important because it creates a multicellular embryo that has organized areas of development.

For humans, these terms are more specific. The first mass of cells produced by a zygote is known as a morula, which then changes into a **blastocyst** (instead of a blastula).

In vertebrates, the next phase of embryonic development is **gastrulation**, in which the ball of cells becomes a three-layered organism. These embryonic tissues are called the ectoderm, endoderm, and mesoderm. The **ectoderm** covers the outside of this three-layered organism except for a small cluster of endoderm cells that eventually become the anus.

In humans, the outer layer is known as the trophoblast (which eventually forms part of the placenta), and the inner cell mass is known as the embryoblast, which has two layers, the hypoblast and epiblast. This ball of cells, which is filled with uterine fluid, implants itself in the uterine wall.

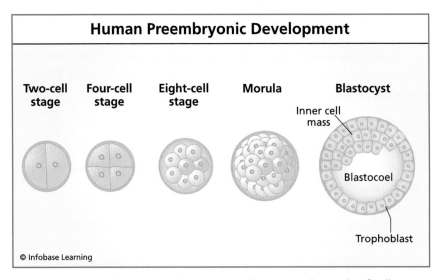

Human Preembryonic Development

Two-cell stage   **Four-cell stage**   **Eight-cell stage**   **Morula**   **Blastocyst**

Inner cell mass

Blastocoel

Trophoblast

© Infobase Learning

FIGURE 3.3 Preembryonic development involves several rounds of cell division. Cleavage involves five cell divisions that give rise to a 32-cell morula. The cells of the morula continue to divide and rearrange themselves into a more rounded and hollow ball-like blastocyst.

The primitive streak then appears—assuring bilateral symmetry of development—and starts germ layer development. The epiblast moves towards the primitive streak and forms a new layer called the **endoderm,** which pushes the hypoblast out of the way. This epiblast eventually forms the **mesoderm** and the top layer is now the ectoderm.

When gastrulation is complete, these distinct layers differentiate into all of the parts of the body through the process of migrating cells. For example, the nervous system and epidermis arise from the ectoderm. The endoderm forms the innermost part of the digestive tract. From the mesoderm, most of the other organs, including the heart, kidney, muscles, and dermis, develop. Also, the notochord develops from the mesoderm, which is the core of the backbone. The neural tube, which is created when the neural folds rise up on either side of the neural plate, becomes the brain and spinal cord. Development is the result of changes in cell shape, migration (movement) of cells, and programmed cell death (such as the death of cells to create the spaces between our fingers). Signals travel between cells (known as the process of induction) to provide instructions for development.

The multicellular human embryo that is formed at one month shares many features with other vertebrates, including a notochord, a head with

EMBRYONIC TISSUE LAYERS AND RESULTING ORGANS AND TISSUES

Each layer of germ tissue corresponds to specific organs and tissues, as shown.

GERM LAYER	DEVELOPED ORGAN AND TISSUE
Ectoderm	Adrenal medulla
	Epithelial lining of mouth and rectum
	Eye: cornea and lens
	Head: connective tissues and hair
	Mammary glands
	Pigment cells
	Nervous system: central nervous system, ganglia, nerves, sensory
	Skin: epidermis and receptors
	Tooth enamel
Mesoderm	Adrenal cortex
	Body cavity lining
	Circulatory system: heart, blood (lymph cells), and spleen
	Excretory system
	Muscular system
	Notochord
	Reproductive system (except for gametes)
	Skeleton
	Skin: dermis
Endoderm	Digestive tract: epithelial lining (except for mouth and rectum)
	Liver

(continues)

Endoderm (continued)	Pancreas
	Parathyroid
	Reproductive system
	Respiratory system: epithelial lining, trachea, bronchi, and air cells of lung
	Thymus
	Thyroid
	Urethra: lining
	Urinary bladder

an eye, limb buds that could develop into either arms and legs or fins, and what appears to be a tail. Still, don't be fooled! The human embryo is definitely different than any other embryo because of its distinctly human genes, the instructions from the genes that will develop the embryo into a human embryo, the release of human chorionic gonadotropin hormone from the embryo, the position of the embryo in a mother's pear-shaped uterus, and much more. At nine weeks, it is clear that the embryo has developed into human fetus.

DEVELOPMENT OF TISSUES, ORGANS, AND SYSTEMS

Along with cell growth and differentiation, cells undergo **morphogenesis** to cause an organism to develop its shape. This process controls the spatial distribution of cells during embryonic development, and may be induced by hormones. As noted previously, induction via signals leads to greater specialization of cells, causing the formation of organs. For example, the brain cells start to bulge outward to become the optic vesicle. This "outpocketing" becomes the optic cup with the optic stalk. The cells that form the inward pocket elongate and eventually become the retina. Neighboring ectoderm cells may be given signals to fold inward and elongate in order to form the cornea and lens of the eye.

As stated, the embryonic cell layers are given signals that cause the development of specific organs through the process of elongation, migration, and programmed cell death that causes inward and outward pocketing of cells and thickening of cells in certain regions.

Similarly, pattern formation helps guide the arrangement of a body part, such as an arm or leg. Positional chemical signals determine which gene will be expressed for the specific body part that is to be formed. Zones of cells provide position information, such as what is to develop in the anterior and posterior directions, via chemical signals to other cells. This formation is likely aided by the fact that humans have bilateral symmetry, a body design in which the body has a right and left half that are mirror images of each other.

TISSUE, ORGAN, AND SYSTEM FUNCTION

Body organization is another key to understanding the functions of cells when they differentiate into organs and body parts. Tissues arise from the embryonic layers to form epithelial tissues, nerve tissues, connective tissues, and muscle tissues. Each tissue is made of specific cells. For instance, a group of cardiac muscle cells comprise cardiac muscle tissue. This cardiac muscle is the heart, which is the main organ of the circulatory system. Organs are body structures that are made of several types of tissues to form a structural and functional unit. An organ system is a group of organs that work together to perform specific activities in the body. The organ systems and the organs that are included in each are as follows:

- *circulatory system:* heart, blood vessels, lymph, and lymph structures
- *digestive system:* mouth, esophagus, stomach, intestines, liver, and pancreas
- *endocrine system:* adrenal, pituitary, thyroid, and other glands
- *integumentary system:* skin, hair, nails, and sweat glands
- *lymphatic/immune system:* lymphatic vessels, lymph nodes, thymus, tonsils, and spleen
- *muscular system:* skeletal muscle, cardiac muscle, and smooth muscle
- *nervous system:* brain, spinal cord, nerves, and sense organs

HOW TO KEEP YOUR CELLS (AND BODY) IN PRIME SHAPE

Aside from genetics, people can maintain optimal health by eating nutritious foods, getting adequate sleep, avoiding alcohol and tobacco, exercising regularly, and practicing good hygiene. When your body is healthy, your cells are healthy as well!

- **Nutrition:** Obesity is a nationwide problem, but recent research has shown that cells age slower if less food is eaten. (In 2008, scientists at St. Louis University found that limiting calories slowed the production of T3, a thyroid hormone found to slow metabolism and speed up aging.) The vitamins and fiber in nutritious foods help prevent cancer cells with their antioxidant properties. Fiber and other nutrient-rich foods also help prevent inflammation, keeping away heart disease, which helps cardiac cells. Foods that are packed with vitamins and minerals help cells operate at their optimal level.
- **Alcohol and Tobacco:** These substances introduce free radicals that can cause cancer cells.
- **Sleep:** Less than adequate sleep depletes energy reserves and puts stress on cells.
- **Exercise:** Regular exercise adds years to a person's life and improves the functions of the cardiovascular, muscular, and respiratory systems and their respective cells. Exercise also improves brain cells by increasing serotonin and norepinephrine levels that aid in decreasing depressive feelings.

- **reproductive system:** reproductive organs, ovaries, and testes
- **respiratory system:** lungs, trachea, and airway
- **skeletal system:** bones, cartilage, and ligaments
- **urinary system:** kidneys, bladder, and ducts

The organs of these eleven body systems work together to keep us healthy by providing the following necessary functions:

- **circulatory system:** transports cells, respiratory gases, and chemical compounds

- **Healthy pregnancy:** The greatest impact that healthy habits have on cells is evident in pregnant women with a developing fetus. A diet rich in folic acid during pregnancy can prevent neural tube disorders of the developing spine, such as spina bifida. Fetal alcohol syndrome can be prevented if mothers do not drink alcohol during pregnancy. Smoking can cause premature delivery, which can result in low birth weight and underdevelopment of a fetus. Mothers who avoid drugs and toxic chemicals, and do not participate in certain activities, such as cleaning cat litter boxes, can prevent certain disabilities in their developing babies. Good habits, such as exercise, by the mother can help promote healthy development of the circulatory, respiratory, and neuromuscular systems in their babies.

- **Proper hygiene:** When we stay clean, we help maintain our integumentary system (the skin) and destroy germs before our immune system is put on the defensive.

- **Cancer screening and prevention:** Wearing sunscreen prevents skin cancer. Other cancers can be prevented or found early with proper screening, including cervical PAP smears and breast mammography in women. Middle-aged adults and seniors should undergo regular screenings for colon and prostate cancer.

It is important to remember that when we maintain good health habits for our body, we are protecting all of the individual cells as well.

- **digestive system:** captures nutrients from ingested food
- **endocrine system:** coordinates and integrates body activities
- **integumentary system:** covers and protects body
- **lymphatic/immune system:** works in conjunction with circulatory system to transport extracellular fluid. The lymph organs aid in immune defense against microbial infection and cancer.
- **muscular system:** produces body movement
- **nervous system:** receives stimuli, processes information, and directs body function
- **reproductive system:** carries out reproduction of human species

- *respiratory system:* captures oxygen and exchanges gases
- *skeletal system:* protects body and provides support for structure and movement
- *urinary system:* removes metabolic wastes from bloodstream

These systems rarely work in isolation. For example, the skeletal, muscular, integumentary, and nervous systems all work together to provide movement, which can protect a body or acquire food for nourishment. The food that is eaten is processed by the digestive tract, the circulatory system, and the urinary system. The air we breathe is used by the respiratory, circulatory, and muscular systems. These organ systems are dependent on each other, and on the proper functioning of the organs, tissues, and cells that comprise the proper balance of functions in the body is known as homeostasis.

4

Immunity: Defending the Cell

Viruses, bacteria, **protozoa**, fungi, and even cancer cells—what can be done to protect our bodies from infection by these invaders? For one, a healthy body has a strong immune system, which we can support through healthy habits such as proper diet, exercise, sufficient sleep, and the avoidance of alcohol, tobacco, and drugs. However, what are the components of our human immune system and how do they function? How does the immune system protect the cells and, thus, the entire body?

THE LYMPHATIC SYSTEM: A BODY SYSTEM DEDICATED TO DEFENSE

The interior of the human body is a major battleground where invaders such as viruses, bacteria, and even cancer cells are fought off. This battleground is called the **immune system** (or **lymphatic system**), and it contains vessels, lymph nodes, thymus, tonsils, appendix, spleen, and bone marrow. **Lymph** itself is similar to interstitial fluid (the fluid that lies between blood and tissues) and carries invading microbes back to the lymph nodes and other lymphatic organs where **macrophages** and lymphocytes await to fight infection. However, this is not the end of the story. The human body is a fortress surrounded by two layers of defense with a detailed strategy for combating infection by microbial invaders. This strategy employs both a nonspecific immune response and a specific immune response.

The strength of the immune system is clear. Of the 100 trillion cells in the adult human body (some estimates put the number between 50 to 75 trillion), 2 trillion of these are the white blood cells of the immune system (other estimates range from 1 to 10 trillion)! There are 100 billion bacteria living in the large intestine alone, most of which are beneficial to the digestive system. While this number is impressive, it's important to know that, in terms of numbers, there are actually more microbes living in our body than there are cells of the human body—in fact, about 10 to 20 times more! Therefore, a complex strategy of the immune system and a hearty response by it are the best defenses against those microorganisms that threaten the body.

NONSPECIFIC IMMUNE RESPONSE: PROTECTING US FROM EXTERNAL THREATS

The first line of defense against infection is known as nonspecific immune response. The skin is a primary barrier to bacteria and viruses. The worn-out cells of the outermost layer, the epidermis, are continually being replaced and replenished with about 1 million skin cells every 40 minutes.

Additionally, the sweat and oils in the skin work to prevent infection, as do the saliva and tears that contain **lysozymes** that attack the cell walls of microorganisms. Mucous membranes in the respiratory and digestive systems—both of which are exposed to the environment—protect the body, as does the cilia (hairs that line the nostrils, respiratory tract, and lungs) that continually beat and sweep the mucus upward. This sweeps the microbes up the respiratory tract, aided by coughing and sniffling. The microbes are then swallowed down into the digestive system where they are destroyed by the stomach acid.

The more persistent germs that enter the body encounter nonspecific defense cells of the body that include the phagocytic white blood cells, the **neutrophils** (the most common type of white blood cell) and **monocytes**. The neutrophils defend the cell by releasing a chemical similar to bleach that destroys both the bacteria and the neutrophil itself.

Macrophages scour the interstitial fluid of the body, eating bacteria and viruses. Cells that are infected or have cancer are attacked by **natural killer cells (NK)**. Amazingly, natural killer cells have the ability to kill cancer cells before they organize into a tumor. However, the body also has to contend with the resiliency of cancer cells.

Antimicrobial proteins, such as interferons and complement proteins, also assist in the nonspecific immune response. **Interferons**, which are proteins that are activated by virus-infected cells, kill the infected cell and then help neighboring cells by diffusing to them in order to aid them. (Interferons have also been used successfully in cancer treatment and have been studied for the treatment of viral infections.) The **complement proteins** float in plasma in their inactive form and help—or complement—other defenders of the immune system. Some functions of complement proteins include creating holes in microbes (single-celled organisms), coating germs so macrophages can destroy the invaders; they also possibly aid in the inflammatory response. When complement proteins encounter bacteria or fungi, they form a membrane attack complex (MAC). When a MAC enters a cell, it creates a hole in the cell membrane that leads to its destruction.

In addition to interferons, other **cytokines,** which are signaling molecules that include **interleukins, chemokines,** and **tumor necrosis factors** (**TNF**), also aid in nonspecific defense responses. Interleukins are secreted by macrophages and lymphocytes. Chemokines assist during an inflammatory response. **Toll-like receptors** and **T cells** secrete TNFs.

INFLAMMATION AND THE ALLERGIC RESPONSE

Just as a bugler stirs up excitement and announces the advancement of troops in war, the inflammatory response mobilizes nonspecific defense forces. When a microorganism invades the surface of the skin (for instance when a disease like malaria enters the body from a mosquito bite), **mast cells** send out chemical alarm signals called **histamines**. This process begins when an allergen causes an immune response in the body. Macrophages degrade the allergen and fragments of it are sent to the T cells, which stimulate B cells to become plasma cells and produce IgE. These antibodies attach to mast cells and the allergen, upon which the mast cells release histamines.

The release of histamines causes the nearby blood vessels to dilate (vasodilation). Blood and **plasma** filled with neutrophils and macrophages flow into the area, which causes the heat, swelling, and tenderness of the infected site. The white blood cells destroy the germs, but they also die in the process. Their remains are eaten and removed by macrophages. (The pus that can be seen at an infected site is mostly a collection of dead neutrophils [the most abundant white blood cells], remains of tissue cells, and dead pathogens.) The plasma that aided in the fight also releases clotting factors that try to contain the infection to the infected area. If the inflammatory response does spread further, the body may respond by sig-naling the brain to cause a fever that can stimulate phagocytosis (that is, cells that eat germs and other cells) and inhibit microorganism growth. Generally, doctors do not consider a fever as being necessarily bad (as long as it is not too high), since it actually may help the body fight the infection

ALLERGIC REACTIONS: WHAT CAN BE DONE?

Why do humans still have allergic reactions despite having an orga-nized defense against pathogens? Recent studies indicate that the immunoglobulin (Ig) known as antibody IgE is to blame. IgE promotes the release of histamine by binding to mast cells. This causes the wide range of allergic responses from itching to anaphylactic shock (a condi-tion that is life threatening to those with extreme allergies). In a genome mapping of a platypus dating back 160 to 300 million years ago and completed in 2008, IgE and another immunoglobulin, IgG, were found. Comparative analysis of the chicken shows only the existence of the immunoglobulin IgY, which is similar to IgE. However, IgY also per-forms the functions of IgG. What does this mean for humans? Why did humans retain both immunoglobulins? Although the basic purpose of retaining the IgE molecule is unknown, at least we know it is the basic reason for the allergic reaction and the cause of the sneezing that accompanies hay fever.

The allergic response can be classified as one of four types of hyper-sensitivity, where an immune response damages its own body. Type I hypersensitivity, which is mediated by IgE, is an immediate, anaphy-lactic reaction. Type II hypersensitivity is called antibody-dependent hypersensitivity, and is controlled by IgG and IgM antibodies. In Type III hypersensitivity, immune complexes, which are formed of **antigens**, complement proteins, and IgG and IgM antibodies are deposited in various tissues. Cell-mediated or delayed-type hypersensitivity is clas-sified as Type IV hypersensitivity. These reactions, which are mediated by T cells, monocytes, and macrophages, can take two to three days to develop. In addition to many autoimmune and infectious diseases, Type IV hypersensitivity is thought to be involved in contact dermatitis and skin allergies, too.

because bacteria do not grow well at high temperatures. Body temperatures above 103°F (39°C), however, are dangerous and temperatures above 105°F (41°C) can cause death.

More serious allergic responses include allergic asthma and anaphylactic shock. In allergic asthma, an allergen IgE response occurs in the

What can be done to prevent or reduce the chance of allergic reactions? In the home, we can dust, vacuum, wash clothes, and clean to prevent pet dander, pollen, dust, and mold build-up. To prevent outdoor environmental allergies from flaring, we can pay attention to pollutant particle counts given on broadcast weather channels. Often, these counts indicate whether certain allergens, such as ragweed, are abundant that day. Hot, dry days also tend to have higher pollutant counts, but there are certain times of year in specific geographic regions when specific allergens may be abundant. It is estimated that about 35 million Americans have outdoor pollen allergies. Other people are allergic to bee stings and should avoid areas where bees are known to build their nests, such as roof eaves and isolated, neglected structures. During certain times of year, such as late summer, bees can become more aggressive as well. For those with food allergies, the best defense is knowledge. Peanut allergies can be particularly life-threatening and cause anaphylactic shock in some people. Certain foods may not contain peanuts, but they may be processed in factories known to carry peanuts. These foods often are candies, baked goods, or cereal. Sometimes the terms allergy and intolerance are used interchangeably, but this is wrong. Although a person may be lactose intolerant, for example, this is generally not a situation that might cause death as an allergy might. Conversely, people with egg allergies can suffer anaphylactic shock, just like a person with a peanut allergy. Allergic rashes can occur from an allergen touching the skin or showing up in something a person ate or drank. For true allergies that cause weepy eyes, runny noses, and worse, people can treat their symptoms with **antihistamines** that are available either over-the-counter or by a prescription from their doctor. Severe allergies need to be treated immediately with an epinephrine ("epi") pen or a trip to the hospital emergency room because the situation can become life-threatening very quickly.

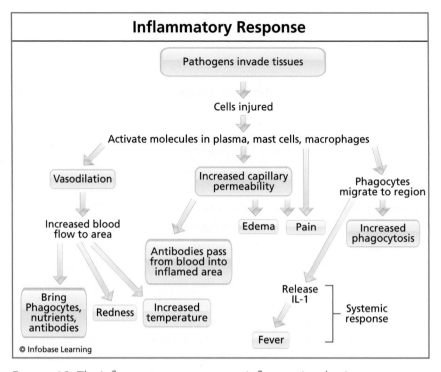

FIGURE 4.1 The inflammatory response, or inflammation, begins immediately after injury. Its processes include vasodilation, increased capillary permeability, and increased phagocytosis.

bronchioles of the lungs. The substances released by the mast cells cause airway constriction.

If the mast cells release large amounts of histamine, so much plasma is lost that the patient goes into anaphylactic shock and can die. Antihistamines are needed immediately, which can be given by an epinephrine injection (known as an "epi" pen, which is carried by most people with severe allergies), to prevent histamine from binding.

THE BODY'S SPECIFIC IMMUNE RESPONSE

In the specific immune response, the immune system steps in to provide focused immunity when the nonspecific response proves to be ineffective. Certain molecules known as antigens are located on the surface of germs, cancer cells, pollens, house dust, and even the cells of transplanted organs. Antibodies that are specific to certain antigens help fight infection. Once the immune system encounters an antigen, a memory of the invader is created, causing an appropriate immune response. It is thought that the body can recognize millions or even billions of antigens. The first time the body encounters an antigen, its defense is just forming (primary immune response), but the next time it appears (secondary immune response), an

HARMFUL IMMUNE RESPONSES

GRAFT REJECTION

Skin that is needed for a skin graft can be taken from one part of the body and placed in another location in the same person or in an identical twin. There is a 95% chance that it will "take" because an identical twin transplant recipient contains the same **MHC antigens** (major histocompatability complex). However, when these antigens are different, an immune response called graft rejection occurs. In the initial stage, T cells known as T_H and T_C recognize the antigens. (T cells are lymphocytes that develop in the thymus and have a CD4 marker.) In another stage, T_C cells, complement proteins, and cytokines from T_H cells attack the transplant and kill it within a week. Therefore, there has to be as close a match as possible. Transplant patients always require the use of anti-rejection drugs. Physicians are developing techniques that use animal tissues for grafts, but they need to be aware of the species-specific diseases that can occur. Doctors are also looking at using organs from genetically-engineered animal organs, or replacing them with artificial organs.

RH INCOMPATIBILITY

Human blood has Rh (rhesus) factors, just like in the rhesus monkeys they were named for. Rh factors are substances found on the surface of red blood cells that cause a strong reaction in certain people who lack the substance. While there are 50 known blood-group antigens, the commonly-known Rh factor refers to the D antigen. If a pregnant woman is Rh-negative and a father is Rh-positive, the fetus may be Rh-positive because it inherits the father's D allele. Consequently, the mother's immune system is activated to make antibodies to antigen D. If the same woman gets pregnant again, D antibodies will be produced by the body and enter the fetal blood, affecting red blood cells and their ability to carry oxygen. Because of the D allele, the baby will be born with jaundice or anemia, as a result of hemolytic disease. If left untreated, the baby may be stillborn or die shortly after birth.

all-out fight occurs, thanks to the **memory cells**. This is the principle at work behind vaccination.

When an antigen is encountered, regardless of whether it is a natural occurrence or a vaccine, it results in **active immunity.** Mothers can provide **passive immunity** to their developing fetuses through their breast milk and getting flu vaccinations themselves.

ARMING THE IMMUNE SYSTEM: THE ROLE OF VACCINES

As mentioned earlier, a vaccination is the injection of a dead or disabled pathogen or a similar, more harmless germ that triggers an immune system response. After this primary immune response, the body produces an imprint of the pathogen onto memory cells to activate a more powerful secondary immune response. In addition to smallpox eradication, there have been many successful vaccination programs, including polio, tetanus, and diphtheria. There are other vaccines for diseases including chicken pox, shingles (known as herpes zoster), measles, mumps, and pneumonia. In 2006, the first **human papillomavirus (HPV)** vaccination was marketed to prevent cervical cancer and certain anal and oral cancers. An influenza virus is developed each year that is specific to the type of flu expected that year. Recent influenza vaccinations have been aimed at the Hong Kong flu and the swine flu (H1N1). Unfortunately, many people do not choose to get inoculated (vaccinated) or do not provide their children with these shots, even when schools require that their students receive them. There may be religious reasons why someone may not get vaccinations, such as being a Christian Scientist. Others may elect to not have their children vaccinated because of concerns about the possible association of vaccinations and autism. However, there are problems with this idea. First, vaccinations no longer contain thimerosal, a mercury-based preservative, which was believed to be associated with the occurrence of autism. Therefore, new cases of autism cannot be linked to the thimerosal contained in vaccinations. Also, the study that supported the relationship between autism and vaccination was shown to have many flaws, so it cannot be used to support this concern. The Food and Drug Administration oversees the safety of all vaccines and is sure to notify healthcare providers as well as patients. The importance of vaccination should be emphasized. The number of patient lives affected and the severity of the diseases that vaccinations prevent should not be overlooked. These diseases took many lives before effective vaccinations were developed!

BREAKING IT DOWN WITH LYMPHOCYTES

The lymphocytes include natural killer (NK) cells, B-cells, and T-cells, which all perform in different ways to provide protection against microorganisms. The NK cells that were described earlier assist nonspecific and specific immune responses by releasing certain enzymes called cytokines, perforins, and granzymes. **Perforins** destroy target cells by poking holes in the surface and allowing **granzymes** to enter, which initiate programmed cell destruction. The **B cells,** which originate in blood marrow and mature into plasma cells, provide humoral immunity (defending the body fluids either through active or passive immunity). T cells originate in the thymus (hence, the term *T cell*) and release TNFs. T cells provide cell-mediated immunity and, as such, the immunity cannot be transferred passively (for example, through a mother's milk). Only an actual cell transfer with T cells can impart immunity to a non-immune person. T cells work in several ways. First, they protect the body from viruses, bacteria, protozoa, and fungi by directly attacking infected cells and may also defend the body against cancer cells. Secondly, T cells provide indirect immunity by signaling other white blood cells to perform phagocytosis and stimulating B cells to produce antibodies. To do this, interleukin-1 submits a signal that causes **helper T cells** to use interleukin-2 to call into action **killer T cells**. These killer T cells have **receptor proteins** on the surface of their cell membranes that recognize bits of viral protein on the surface of infected cells and then puncture the cell membranes to kill those cells. (Puncturing the cell membrane allows water to rush into the cell, which causes the cell to burst.) Also, the interleukin-2 simultaneously activates the B cells, which also have receptor proteins on their surface that are called antibodies. The B cells release the antibodies to attach to the pathogens, but the B cells do not directly attack the pathogens or the infected cells themselves. Instead, the antibodies released by the B cells signal the activation of macrophages and natural killer cells.

Both B cells and T cells develop antigen receptors on the surface of each cell that recognize a specific antigen and launch an appropriate attack. Scientists believe that the human body contains anywhere from 100 million to 100 billion B cells and T cells that can fight virtually any infection. Likewise, the antigens have certain areas on them called **antigenic determinants** where antibodies bind to them. When an antigen enters the body and activates a small number of lymphocytes into action, clones of these B cells and T cells are made.

(continues on page 60)

WHY VACCINATIONS MATTER

Diseases used to wipe out a good portion of the population around the world in global epidemics known as pandemics. Luckily, major illnesses don't happen as often today in most of the developed world. However, countries of the developing world, such as those in Africa, are still affected by many diseases. This is due to poor sanitation and water systems, the tropical climate, and a lack of vaccination programs in those countries.

Vaccinations are created from weakened or dead versions of antigens of diseases. In some cases, they may even be made of similar antigens that cause less severe reaction than the actual disease itself (for example, cowpox for smallpox). Vaccinations should be started in infancy, and actually even sooner. Pregnant women should receive influenza vaccines to provide passive immunity to their fetuses. Several important vaccinations are needed before a child turns six years old, including vaccinations for measles, mumps, whooping cough, rubella, tetanus, chicken pox, and others. Adolescents need other vaccinations and boosters (repeated vaccine injections), including ones for HPV and tetanus. Adults still need to keep up with vaccinations, either as boosters (for example, tetanus), or when they are traveling to areas of the world known to carry certain diseases that are not often found where they live.

Here are some of the diseases that have been either eliminated or reduced by the use of vaccinations:

- bacterial meningitis (*Haemophilus influenzae* type b [Hib], *neisseria meningitidis*, and *Streptococcus pneumoniae*)
- bubonic plague
- chicken pox (Varicella)
- diphtheria
- hepatitis A and B
- human papillomavirus/cervical cancer
- influenza (multiple variants, including swine flu [H1N1])
- measles

- mumps
- pneumonia
- polio
- rabies (only following contact with animals with suspected illness)
- rotavirus
- rubella (German measles)
- shingles (zoster)
- smallpox
- tetanus
- typhoid
- whooping cough

Vaccinations for the following diseases are needed for travel to tropical regions and specific countries.

- cholera
- hepatitis A and B
- polio
- typhoid fever
- typhus
- yellow fever

After a disease has been completely eliminated from the world, a decision that is based on known cases, vaccinations are no longer needed for the prevention of the disease—such is the case for smallpox. Some people question whether to continue providing the polio vaccine once the world has been vaccinated. Still, it would take only one case for the illness to be reintroduced to the entire world. Following the successful creation of the HPV vaccine to prevent cervical cancer, drug companies are continuing to research and develop vaccinations for many diseases. (However, the drug companies have not been making similar efforts to develop new antibiotics.) Some of the diseases they are working to prevent include the sexually transmitted diseases of HIV/AIDS, syphilis, and chlamydia, as well as malaria and other tropical diseases.

(continued from page 57)

WHEN THE IMMUNE SYSTEM MALFUNCTIONS OR FAILS

The main reason for an inadequate immune system response is because of an **autoimmune disease**. In that disease process, the body cannot distinguish between its own cells and that of a foreign invader. As a result, the immune system goes haywire and attacks the body's own molecules. Specifically, T cells react against a body's own cells through the overactivation of T cells and B cells, which causes inflammation and autoimmune disease. Conversely, if there is decreased activation of T cells and B cells in the body, this can allow pathogens to cause disease.

Often a viral or bacterial infection comes before an autoimmune disease shows itself. Unfortunately, pathogens are crafty and can produce molecules that disguise themselves as molecules that already exist in the body without causing harm. For instance, the adenovirus that causes respiratory and gastrointestinal illnesses also produces a molecule that looks like the myelin protein found in nerves. Therefore, when the body attacks the virus, it may also attack the myelin of nerves, as well. This can result in an autoimmune disease like multiple sclerosis, in which antibodies attack the glial cells that produce myelin.

Autoimmune diseases typically strike between the ages of 20 and 40 years, but they also can occur in people with a family history of the disease or those from certain ethnic backgrounds. Systemic lupus erythematosus (popularly known as "lupus") is an autoimmune disease of B cell hyperactivity. Lupus occurs more frequently in women than in men, especially in those between the ages of 15 to 35. It also appears to be more frequent in people of non-European descent. Another autoimmune disease, plaque psoriasis, is a skin condition that can affect most areas of the body, including under the nails, and also evolve into psoriatic arthritis. Psoriasis has been classified as an autoimmune disease in which helper T cells become overactive. Although it initially affects those between the ages of 15 and 25, it can strike children as well.

Autoimmune diseases also include, but are not limited to, Type 1 diabetes, Graves' disease, rheumatoid arthritis, and Guillain-Barré syndrome. Several body systems are affected by autoimmune disease. In the

Opposite: FIGURE 4.2 The two primary kinds of immune system cells are lymphocytes (T cells and B cells) and antigen-presenting cells (macrophages and dendritic cells). They interact via complex signaling.

Immune System Cells

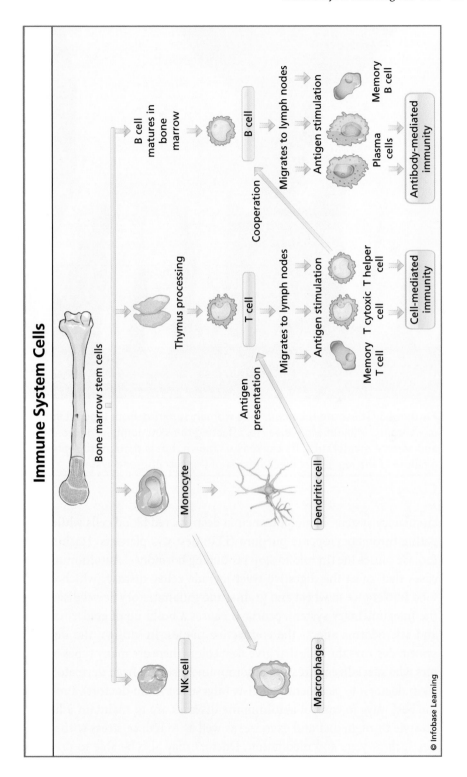

Bone marrow stem cells

NK cell

Monocyte

Macrophage

Dendritic cell

Antigen presentation

Thymus processing

T cell

Migrates to lymph nodes

Antigen stimulation

Memory T cell   cytotoxic T cell   T helper cell

Cell-mediated immunity

B cell matures in bone marrow

B cell

Cooperation

Migrates to lymph nodes

Antigen stimulation

Plasma cells   Memory B cell

Antibody-mediated immunity

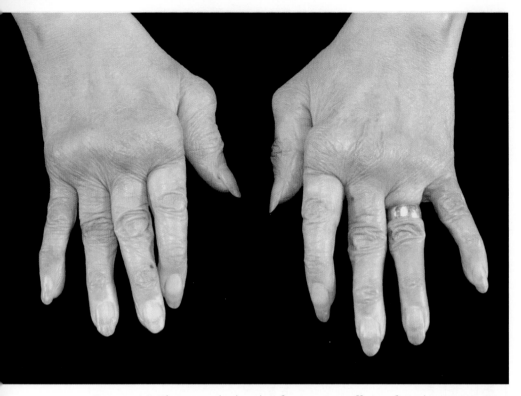

FIGURE 4.3 These are the hands of a woman suffering from lupus. Lupus is a chronic, inflammatory disease, affecting the skin, joints, kidneys, heart, and serosal membranes. Its cause is unknown, but is thought to represent a failure of the regulatory mechanisms of the autoimmune system.

circulatory system, hemolytic anemia destroys red blood cells while idiopathic thrombocytopenic purpura (ITP) destroys platelets. Hashimoto's disease causes the thyroid to stop producing hormones. Autoimmune diseases that affect the digestive tract include celiac disease (which causes food intolerance to wheat and grains) and inflammatory bowel disease. In the integumentary system, psoriasis causes a build-up of epidermal cells and scleroderma affects the connective tissues. In vitiligo, the immune system destroys the cells that give skin color. There are many types of doctors who specialize in treating autoimmune diseases, from dermatologists (skin doctors) to gastroenterologists (digestive system doctors). Presently, the best ways to control autoimmune diseases are to maintain a healthy lifestyle through diet and exercise, as well as to reduce stress with activities such as yoga and meditation. Doctors may also be able to prescribe

ARE HUMANS RESISTANT TO DISEASES THAT CAUSED HARM IN THE PAST?

The campaign to vaccinate large populations of people against small-pox has resulted in the complete eradication of the disease, the first known eradication of a disease by humans. This raises the question of whether humans have successfully conquered other illnesses through the course of natural selection via evolution. Are humans now resistant to diseases that caused them harm in the past? Several different types of research from studies in live animals and humans (known as *in vivo*), genetic research, and microbiology indicate that humans may have become resistant to certain diseases that would have caused disease or death in the past.

This evolutionary process of immunity to certain diseases is ongoing, as noted in a study presented in 2010 by researcher Jean Casanova. In his study of invasive pneumococcal disease and herpes simplex encephalitis, Casanova presented evidence that the extent of disease infection is dependent upon an individual's genetic make-up. If a person has a weak immune system to a particular pathogen, there is a stronger chance that he will develop a disease. A genetic evolution in disease resistance also was noted in 2010 in another study by scientists in England. In that study, the residents of some of the oldest cities in the world had a genetic variant (change in composition) that provided greater immunity to diseases such tuberculosis and leprosy. However, other researchers in the fields of microbiology believe that the likelihood of catching a disease is only based on environmental factors. Regardless, this ability to withstand microbial offenders fits in with the theory of evolution, with survival of the fittest prevailing.

The ability to adapt and evolve in response to an outside threat is apparent in the research of diseases. For example, people of African descent carry the genetic trait for sickle cell anemia. This disease causes red blood cells (**hemoglobin**) to form into a shape that is unable to carry oxygen in the bloodstream. This feature is thought to be the result of the red blood cell adapting to the threat of a specific type of malaria through mutation in accordance with natural selection. This sickle cell trait provides a survival advantage over people who have normal hemoglobin for

(continues)

(continued)

this type of malaria in areas where there are malaria epidemics. However, those with this trait also have to contend with the serious effects of sickle cell anemia. Although humans are able to vaccinate against, treat, and possibly eradicate diseases that have long plagued our species, unfortunately, new diseases arise to challenge scientists. This has been the case with HIV, which causes AIDS, as well as hantavirus, Ebola virus, and others. Unfortunately, this is nothing new. When settlers from England and Europe arrived in North America, they brought along a host of new illnesses to the Native Americans.

treatments to relieve symptoms and suppress the immune system from over-functioning. However, this suppression by medications comes at a cost, and may cause other illnesses to develop because of lowered immunity response.

Other malfunctions of the immune system are not autoimmune, but are the result of immunodeficiency. This means that a component of the immune system is missing or not functioning. Acquired immunodeficiency diseases that totally disable the immune system include HIV and AIDS. Allergies and transplant organ rejection also represent the overreaction of the immune system to an outside threat. The memory of an outside invader assists in the immune response to the microbe the following year, but it does not always provide the same protection against similar pathogens. The immune system may respond appropriately and well to one type of influenza virus vaccine, but the next year it does not have an immune response to the new version of the flu. Finally, the simple common cold virus is not so simple for the immune system to defend against or cure.

5

Unseen Enemies: Bacterial, Viral, Fungal, and Parasitic Threats

Specific types of microorganisms cause illnesses in humans. These types include viruses, prokaryotic bacteria, eukaryotic fungi, protists, and parasitic worms. (Recall that prokaryotic means that the bacteria do not have a distinctive nucleus, and eukaryotic means the microbe has a nucleus and cell membranes.) What follows is a discussion about the features of each of these microorganisms and the unique ability of each to overpower the human cell.

VIRUSES

What are Viruses?

Viruses are much larger than bacteria. They range in size from the very small polio virus, which measures around 20 nanometers (nm), to the rather large smallpox virus, which measures around 400 nm. Viruses are still incredibly tiny, though. (By comparison, sperm, the smallest cell in the human body, measures 2 μm, which is two-millionths of a meter. A virus is measured in nanometers, which is one-billionth of a meter.) Another feature of viruses is that they cannot live for long outside the host cell, unlike bacteria.

French scientist Louis Pasteur was among the first to explore the origin of the virus that causes rabies. However, the first virus was isolated by Martinus Beijerinck in 1898, one that affected the tobacco plant. Over the years, there has been much debate whether viruses are actual living organisms. One indication that they are living organisms is that they have nuclei that allow them to replicate. They are also contained by an outside protein capsid (a cell membranelike structure) that also may contain carbohydrates, lipids, and trace metals. Protein subunits of the capsid determine the shape of the virus: helical, polyhedral (meaning a three-dimensional shape with many flat edges and lines, such as

INFLUENZA: THE EVER-CHANGING THREAT

Commonly known as the flu, influenza is a common viral threat that arises each year despite new and updated vaccinations. Why is this so? Why do strains of the flu differ from year to year? How do we try to keep ahead of the next version? Why do we get the flu in spite of having a vaccine? Why do some people appear to get sick with the flu after a vaccine?

The influenza virus is a resilient and adaptive microorganism that causes serious illness. Flu symptoms include fever, chills, sore throat, runny or stuffy nose, headache, and tiredness (but usually not the vomiting and diarrhea typically associated with gastrointestinal flu, a condition known as enteritis). Complications of the flu include pneumonia, bronchitis, and sinus and ear infections. Each year, before the height of influenza season, scientists from the Centers of Disease Control (CDC) along with the WHO determine from lab samples and epidemiological studies where and what the next strain of influenza virus will be for the upcoming year. These are best-guess estimates that result in quick production of vaccines by drug companies for that strain. However, sometimes these estimates are wrong, and another strain emerges to cause most flu cases that year. The vaccination that was developed and given will only provide immunity to the strains that are in it, and no other. Also, sometimes not enough vaccinations are available or people choose not to get vaccinated in time to protect themselves from infection. People will get sick with influenza if they do not have immunity to a particular new strain. It takes up to two weeks adenoviruses), or a combination of a polyhedral shape with a tail (the shape of a virus known as a bacteriophage).

However, viruses are **acellular**. This means they have no metabolism (the production and use of energy) or respiration (breathing). These actions are basic functions of life. So, can something without these basic functions be called life?

following vaccination for people to develop full immunity. If flu symptoms arise within 48 hours of the vaccination, it is usually a mild reaction to the dead virus cells that are used to elicit an immune response and not full-blown flu.

Some recent influenza variants have come from Asia and Mexico. Typically, flu strains are named for either their apparent geographic origin, such as Asian flu, Hong Kong flu, and Spanish flu, or for the source, for example, avian flu or **swine flu (H1N1)**. (There are some misconceptions about naming an influenza strain for an animal, though.) As mentioned, most viruses are species specific. It is only when an influenza virus jumps from an animal to a human and then co-mingles with a human influenza strain that a new strain appears. Therefore, safe hygiene practices when handling animals, along with proper slaughter and cooking practices, are warranted. However, most of us get the flu from another infected human, and probably not directly from a pig or bird.

Influenza viruses are categorized as Types A, B, or C. The reason why the Type A influenza virus changes each year is due to antigenic drift and antigenic shift. In antigenic drift, small mutations occur for which humans are partially immune. In antigenic shift, the pathogen changes through the combination of two or more influenza strains. The changes in Type B influenza are smaller, slower, and species specific to humans and seals. Type C influenza affects humans and pigs, but is not the Type A swine flu (H1N1). Types A and C influenza are capable of causing epidemics in humans. Although tests are available to identify the type and strain of influenza, doctors are more likely to treat a patient's immediate symptoms rather than run tests to identify the variant, unless such tests are requested by a health organization.

As mentioned, though, the virus does have a nucleus, which can be either DNA or RNA, but not both. This genetic material can be single-stranded (ssDNA or ssRNA) or double-stranded (dsDNA or dsRNA).

Viruses reproduce by using their genetic material to force the host cell to reproduce their viral nucleic acid. DNA viruses include poxviruses (which causes diseases like smallpox), herpesesviruses (cold sores, genital herpes, and shingles), papillomaviruses (including those that cause warts and cervical cancer), and parvoviruses (gastroenteritis). RNA viruses include picornaviruses (which cause polio, hepatitis A, and the common cold), togaviruses (rubella), orthomyxoviruses (influenza), paramyxoviruses (measles and mumps), rhabdoviruses (rabies), coronaviruses (upper respiratory infections and severe acute respiratory syndrome, or SARS), flaviviruses (yellow fever, West Nile virus, and hepatitis C), filoviruses (the Ebola virus), bunyaviruses (encephalitis and hantavirus), reoviruses (which cause vomiting, diarrhea, and encephalitis), and retroviruses (AIDS and cancers). However, retroviruses are unique because they contain reverse transcriptase—a DNA polymerase enzyme that transcribes the RNA genome into DNA.

Since viruses don't have many of the features of other living organisms, they cannot be classified in the same way. They are classified in special groups according to their common, shared characteristics, including type of nucleic acid and presence or absence of a capsid.

Where Did Viruses Come From?

The most popular theory is that viruses arose from bits of nucleic acid that escaped from the cells of living organisms and entered other cells through their damaged cell membranes. This escaped gene hypothesis is supported by the fact that many viruses are species specific. In other words, many viruses can only be passed from one human to another human, and not from a human to a dog, for instance. Others suggest that viruses arose from early versions of cells. Despite supporting evidence for this idea, this is unlikely, given that viruses need their host cell to survive. So, how can they have arisen before their host and survived?

The Bacteriophage: A Special Virus

As we will discover in the discussion of bacteria, not all viruses are bad. Bacteriophages are viruses that attack bacteria. They have a complex structure of double-stranded DNA that is usually located in a polyhedral head with a tail that can attach to bacteria. Bacteriophages were used to combat bacterial infections before the discovery of antibiotics.

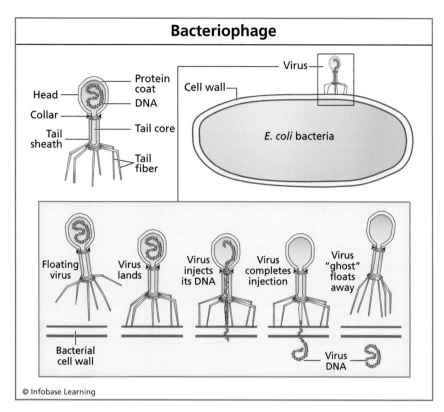

FIGURE 5.1   Bacteriophages settle on the cell wall of a bacterial cell and inject their DNA or RNA into the cell.

Now, because of the emergence of bacteria that are antibiotic resistant, scientists are revisiting bacteriophages and genetically engineering them as possible treatment for resistant bacterial infections. Bacteriophages can also be used to improve food safety, particularly against the common *Escherichia coli.*

How Do Viruses Infect Cells?

Viruses infect cells through their ability to take over a host cell and use their nucleic acids to force the host cell to reproduce new viruses. There are two types of viral reproduction: the lytic cycle and the lysogenic cycle.

In the lytic cycle, a virulent pathogen destroys the host cell in a series of five steps:

1. Attachment, during which the virus first attaches to the host cell wall.

2. Penetration, during which the nucleic acid produced by the virus enters the cell. If the virus is a bacteriophage, then its capsid stays outside, but some viruses enter the cell all at once.
3. Replication and synthesis, during which the virus degrades the host's nucleic acid and synthesizes new viruses.
4. Assembly, in which the components are made into new viruses.
5. Finally, the newly assembled viruses are released from the cell.

Bacteriophages release all at once, but other animal viruses are released slowly. Other viruses bud off the first infected host cell. Viral reproduction can take from less than 20 minutes to more than one hour.

Another type of viral reproduction occurs in the lysogenic cycle. These pathogens don't necessarily destroy their host cell, but rather the virus genome is joined with the host bacterial DNA to create a virus genome called a prophage. When the bacterial DNA replicates, so does the prophage. Lysogenic cells are bacteria with prophages. Despite not being known for destroying the host cells, lysogenic cells are known to change and return back to start a lytic cycle. Also, lysogenic cells can display entirely new properties upon conversion. The ability to code for both the features of the phage and the bacterium are seen in diphtheria and botulism. The attachment proteins on the surface of the virus determine the type of cell, species, and location in the body that it can affect.

WHAT ARE BACTERIA?

As noted previously, each human hosts an abundance of bacteria—more than 20 times the number of cells in a body. Luckily, not all bacteria are pathogens that cause disease. Many bacteria are beneficial. They help break down food and protect our stomachs and digestive system from erosion by our own stomach acid. It is estimated that there are five million trillion trillion bacteria in the world, that is, 5 with 30 zeroes following it (and that doesn't even take into account all the other microorganisms). Bacteria are beneficial to the environment because they break down waste. Without bacteria, dead vegetation and animals would not decompose into vital nutrients and chemical elements such as nitrogen. Scientists have successfully created genetically engineered cyanobacteria that secrete diesel fuel or ethanol in the presence of sunlight, water, and carbon dioxide. (However, certain issues with production and collection need to be solved before this can be an effective alternative to fossil fuel or ethanol made from corn.)

Bacteria are single-celled microorganisms that are prokaryotic (meaning they do not have a distinct nucleus) and mostly heterotrophic (meaning they must obtain their food from an outside source). Bacteria can be spherical cocci, rod-shaped bacilli, spiral-shaped spirilla, comma-shaped vibrio, and tightly coiled spirochete. Although bacteria are microscopic, they are larger than viruses. They are also distinguished by how they exist. Some can exist as single cells, while those that form pairs are *Neisseria*. Other groupings include *Streptococcus*, which forms chains, and *Staphylococcus*, which has the appearance of a cluster of grapes. Actinobacteria are elongated and form filaments. A sheath of individualized cells covers filamentous bacteria and *Nocardia* form complex, branched filaments.

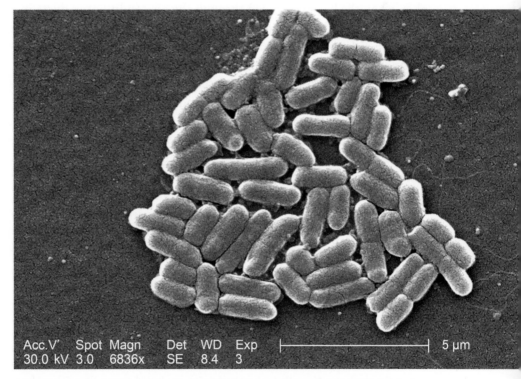

Acc.V Spot Magn   Det   WD   Exp ├────────────────────┤ 5 μm
30.0 kV 3.0 6836x   SE   8.4   3

FIGURE 5.2 This colorized scanning electron micrograph (magnified 6,836 times) shows a number of Gram-negative *E. coli* bacteria of the strain O157:H7, which is one of hundreds of strains of this bacterium. Although most strains are harmless and live in the intestines of healthy humans and animals, this strain produces a powerful toxin, which can cause severe illness. This strain of *E. coli* was first recognized as a cause of illness in 1982 during an outbreak of severe bloody diarrhea that was traced to contaminated hamburgers.

Another distinction between bacteria is their different types of cell walls, which can be classified as Gram-positive and Gram-negative. **Gram staining** is a technique that differentiates bacteria into one of two groups, based on the presence of high levels of peptidoglycan, and is used for identification of the type of bacteria. When something is Gram-positive, it stains a purple-blue color. When something is Gram-negative, it stains pink or red. Some **Gram-positive bacteria** include *Bacillus*, *Clostridium*, and *Heliobacterium*. One major group of **Gram-negative bacteria**, the proteobacteria, includes *Escherichia coli* (*E. coli*), *Salmonella*, and *Shigella*. Another Gram-negative bacterium is *Legionella*. In 1976, the first outbreak of Legionnaire's disease (*Legionella*) in the United States struck American Legion group members in Philadelphia, when the bacteria spread through the air conditioning ducts in a hotel. Before the disease and antibiotic for treatment were identified, the pathogen sickened many and killed two who were affected by pneumonia and fevers above 107° F (41.6°C).

In humans, the Gram-negative cocci *Neisseria gonorrhoeae* causes the sexually transmitted disease gonorrhea and *Neisseria meningitidis* causes meningitis. Gram-negative bacilli cause a variety of respiratory problems, as well as urinary and gastrointestinal problems. Many illnesses that are contracted during hospital stays are caused by Gram-negative bacteria, including *Acinetobacter baumannii*, which causes bacteremia, secondary meningitis, and ventilator-associated pneumonia.

Endospores are unique in that they can remain dormant for a very long period of time, even in conditions of extreme dryness or high temperatures. When environmental conditions are suitable for growth, the endospore germinates. An example of such an endospore is *Clostridium tentani* which causes the illness called tetanus (also known as lockjaw).

Bacteria Structure

While the outside of different types of bacteria may have unique features, like flagella (tail), their interior structure is similar. Unlike animal eukaryotic cells, prokaryotic cells lack membrane-enclosed organelles. Therefore, there are no nuclei, mitochondria, endoplasmic reticula, Golgi complexes, or lysosomes. Instead, a cell wall encapsulates a prokaryote's insides, which include DNA, ribosomes, storage granules, and plasma membrane. Some bacteria also produce a capsule or slime layer around the cell wall. In addition to the DNA, most bacteria have their genetic information stored in plasmids, which are circular fragments of genetic material.

Bacteria Reproduction

Bacteria are extremely versatile and so abundant that it is clear that their reproduction happens efficiently and quickly. Bacteria mainly reproduce asexually by **binary fission**. This means that one cell divides into similar cells when circular DNA replicates and then a transverse wall is formed.

The transfer of genetic information occurs in three primary ways. It may be through transformation (in which DNA fragments released by one cell are taken in by another), transduction (a phage takes bacterial genes into another bacteria), or conjugation (contact between two different cells results in an exchange of genetic information).

How Do Bacteria Infect Cells?

When we get sick, it is the result of **exotoxins** that are secreted by some living bacteria. These exotoxins travel through the bloodstream and target tissues. Botulism, for example, is a type of food poisoning that is caused by the exotoxin of *Clostridium botulinum*. In Gram-negative bacteria, **endotoxins** are contained in cell walls that are released from dead bacteria. When endotoxins bind to the host's macrophages, widespread symptoms, such as fever, are felt by the infected person. Unlike exotoxins, endotoxins cannot be destroyed by heating.

WHAT ARE PROTISTS?

Protists are simple, unicellular eukaryotic microorganisms, many of which cause parasitic diseases in their hosts. They have various structures that help them move about, including flagella, cilia, and pseudopodia (temporary extension used for feeding and movement in amoebas). They are known to cause serious intestinal diseases, such as dysentery. Although some of these illnesses primarily originate in tropical areas, other parasitic diseases, such as trichomoniasis, a rather common sexually transmitted disease, do not.

Diseases such as malaria and sleeping sickness are spread by certain flying insects, including mosquitoes and flies. Malaria is a parasitic, spore-forming protist that doesn't have structures for locomotion, but instead uses microtubules to attach to its host. Malaria is particularly troublesome because it is becoming resistant to antimalarial drugs and pesticides. Toxoplasmosis from cat urine can result in mental retardation in unborn fetuses, so pregnant women must avoid cleaning cat litter boxes. Another illness caused by protists is backpacker's diarrhea

(*Giardia intestinalis*), which is caused by drinking untreated water from wilderness streams.

WHAT ARE FUNGI?

If there is a fungus among us, it might well infect us. A **fungus** is a eukaryotic microorganism that is heterotrophic. Its cell walls are made of chitin,

THE BLACK DEATH

Occurring from 1348 to 1350, the Black Death, or bubonic plague that struck Europe, was perhaps the most destructive pandemic (worldwide epidemic) in history. The Black Death is believed to have been caused by *Yersinias pestis*, bacteria from the fleas of infected rats inadvertently brought from China. During the epidemic, the rates of bubonic plague were so high that an estimated 30% to 60% of Europe's population died. The close living quarters, poor sanitation and hygiene, and lack of antibiotics were major reasons for the rapid spread of the disease. The spread was caused by fleas that passed from rat to human and infected people who coughed on others. Much prejudice and mistreatment of certain ethnic groups, including Jews and Gypsies, occurred as a result of the plague because these groups of people either lived in poorer conditions or apart from the mainstream population.

Although we think of bubonic plague as a disease of the Middle Ages, it is still around, but to a much lesser extent. Outbreaks have occurred again at various times throughout the world, including the United States. The last major epidemic in Los Angeles was in the 1920s, but isolated cases were later reported in California, Nevada, New Mexico, Arizona, Colorado, and Oregon, according to the CDC. Around 1,000 to 3,000 cases of plague are reported yearly by WHO. Cases have occurred in recent history in South America, Africa, and Asia. Improved methods of sanitation, hygiene, and extermination of rodents have helped decrease the number of cases. Risk factors for plague are exposure to flea bites from rodents and prairie dogs, and scratches and bites from infected domestic cats, according to the U.S. National Institutes of Health.

a substance that also comprises the exoskeleton of insects. Fungi usually have a filamentlike shape, and reproduce by spores. These spores spread by wind, water, or animals. Most fungi are involved in decomposition of elements, but some of them are parasites. Fungi are beneficial to humans as part of our beverages and food, such as mushrooms and cheese. Also, they are extremely useful as medicines, such as penicillin and statins.

The most significant factor in the reduction of plague has been the introduction of antibiotics. Prompt attention is needed whenever someone is infected by plague because of its reportedly extremely high death rate—near 90%—for infected people who fail to get help within the first 24 hours. Unfortunately, if the antibiotics that are currently used to treat plague today become ineffective and suitable conditions arise, particularly in urban areas, the chance for a worldwide epidemic of bubonic plague is still possible.

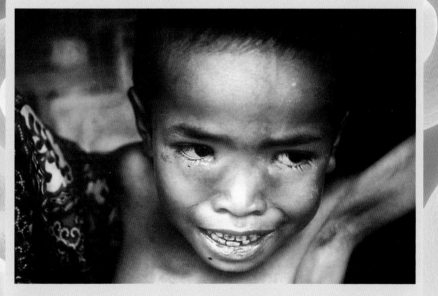

FIGURE 5.3 A young boy has a bubo—an inflamed, swollen lymph node—under his left armpit and similar swelling near his eyes (bilateral lacrimal glands). Bubonic plague occurs when an infected flea bites a person allowing *Y. pestis* bacteria to enter through an opening in skin.

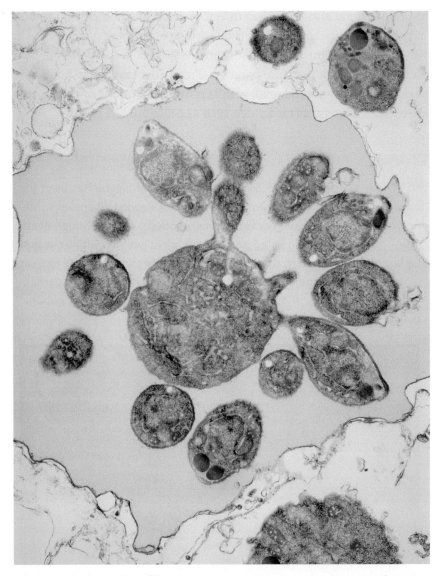

FIGURE 5.4 *Plasmodium falciparum*, a protozoan parasite, causes malaria in humans.

However, fungi can also cause serious illnesses, including candidiasis (yeast infections) and histoplasmosis (lung infections). Of the fungi known as mycotoxins, aflatoxin is known to cause cancer in humans. Trace amounts of it can be found on peanuts, corn, and meat. Doctors prescribe antifungals to cure fungal infections.

CHALLENGING IMMUNITY: THE POWER OF BACTERIA AND VIRUSES

The immune system is a powerful force against infectious microbials. This chapter discusses the various pathogens. In a show of survival of the fittest, these microorganisms have adapted to where they are able to overpower the immune system. Viruses are adept at mutation through antigenic drift and antigenic shift. Bacteria, protists, and fungi have recently shown drug resistance. Luckily, over the course of history, global health organizations have created better and more organized resources to identify these threats and are working with pharmaceutical and biotechnology companies to develop new and improved drugs and methods to control and possibly destroy diseases.

6

Genetics: When "Family Traditions" Can Be Harmful

HOW GENES CONTROL HUMAN CELL FUNCTIONS AND CHARACTERISTICS

Genes serve as "ground control" for each one of our cells. They command the functions and characteristics of cells. To understand how genetic messages become disrupted, it is important to know how traits—such as tendencies toward certain diseases—are passed on via the genes and the processes that are involved.

TYPES OF INHERITANCE

Once a zygote forms through the union of a man and woman during sexual reproduction, the developing fetus that results is unique because of the particular DNA that has been provided by both the man and the woman, as well as the selective expression of only certain genes. Certain types of inherited traits are known. These are autosomal dominant inheritance, autosomal recessive inheritance, and sex-linked inheritance.

Autosomal dominant inheritance is a basic pattern of inheritance where a defect in only one of the two alleles (forms) of a gene leads to a disorder that comes from one parent. It is also known as a "gain of function." When the defective allele is coded on an autosome (a chromosome that isn't a sex chromosome), this causes an autosomal dominant disorder. Some autosomal dominant disorders include Huntington's disease (which causes neurological problems), hydrocephalus (which is manifested by a swelling brain and mental retardation), and Williams syndrome (also known as Williams-Beuren syndrome, which features mental retardation and speech problems).

In **autosomal recessive inheritance**, disorders are caused by a defect in both alleles of a gene. This means that an affected person must have inherited a defective allele from each parent. This produces a "loss of function" because a loss of both copies is needed to manifest the disorder. When the defective alleles are coded on an autosome, this causes an autosomal recessive disorder. Certain populations may have more autosomal recessive carriers because of the founder effect and selective advantage. **Founder effect** is where a defective allele is found more frequently in a subset of descendants of a general population. This defective allele appears in a population that was founded by a few individuals with a carrier in their group after they broke off from the main group. Another population-specific trend of inheritance is selective advantage. If a defective allele improves a carrier's chances for survival, then that allele will appear more frequently in descendants than in the general population. One example of this is sickle cell anemia. (As noted previously, this trait affects red blood cells and protects against malaria, but it causes other symptoms as a result.)

There are many examples of diseases caused by autosomal recessive inheritance, including Tay-Sachs disease (which only affects people from a certain population of Jewish ancestry) and PKU (phenylketonuria, which is tested for in newborn infants). PKU is found in offspring who express the genetically-inherited autosomal recessive gene, but the frequency of the disease is higher among those born in Italy and China.

Sex-linked inheritance is a form of inheritance where genes are coded on sex chromosomes from both the mother (X-linked inheritance) and the father (Y-linked inheritance). The reason why X-linked inheritance can only occur from mothers is that fathers only have one X-chromosome. Comparatively, only fathers can contribute to Y-linked inheritance because only men have a Y-chromosome. Both female and male offspring can have an X-linked disorder, but only sons can have a Y-linked disorder. **X-linked dominant disorders** include RETT syndrome, which almost exclusively affects girls and may be misdiagnosed as cerebral palsy. Only males are affected by Fragile X syndrome, which is a common form of mental retardation and autism spectrum disorder. There are also **X-linked recessive disorders,** which almost only

(continues on page 82)

WHAT ARE MY ODDS?

The following is a brief guide to show the likelihood of inheriting a genetic disorder.

Autosomal dominant disorder: The person affected by the disorder has at least one affected parent.

- An affected parent (with one affected allele) coupled with an unaffected parent will have an equal number of affected and unaffected children (on average).
- Unaffected children of affected parents have unaffected children and grandchildren.

Autosomal recessive disorder: Affected person must have a defective allele from each parent.

- If unaffected parents have an affected child, then both parents are carriers, each with a copy of the defective allele.
  - Children of two carriers are, on average, one-fourth affected, one-fourth unaffected, and one-half unaffected carriers.
  - All children of affected parent (with both affected alleles) plus an unaffected parent are unaffected carriers.
  - All children of two affected parents are affected.
  - Males and females are equally likely to be affected.

X-linked dominant disorder: Affected males transmit the disorder to all daughters but not their sons (because fathers contribute the X chromosome to daughters but not to sons).

- Affected females (with one defective allele of a dominant disorder) will transmit the disorder to one-half of their children, with males and females equally affected.
- Some of those afflicted have both alleles affected (even though only one affected allele is enough to cause a disorder.

X-linked recessive disorders: Nearly all those affected are male who, in turn, never transmit the disorder to their sons, but all of whose daughters will be carriers.

(continues)

Opposite: Figure. 6.1 Sex-linked genetic disorders include X-linked dominant disorders and recessive disorders. In X-linked dominant disorders, affected females transmit the disorder to one half of their children. Affected males transmit the disorder only to daughters.

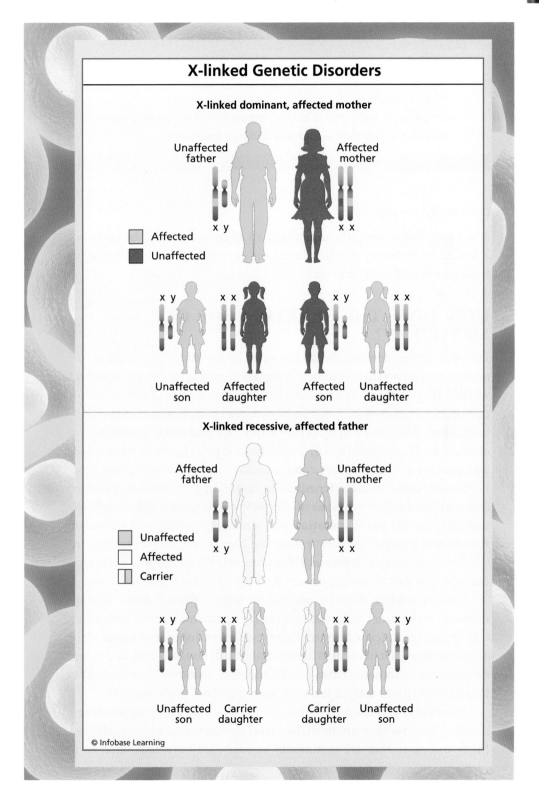

(continued)

- Carrier females will transmit the disorder to half of their sons.
- Half of daughters of carrier females will be carriers.
- An affected male and a carrier female will, on average, transmit disorder to half their daughters and half their sons

(continued from page 82)

affect sons, but almost all daughters of an affected male will be carriers. X-linked inheritance, whether dominant or recessive, cannot be passed from an affected male to a son.

HOW DOES THE GENETIC CODE GET MESSED UP?

Disorders in the genetic code can be caused by mutations in a single chromosome or in two chromosomes. A mutation may arise from a **deletion**, which is the loss of part or an entire chromosome or a loss of DNA nucleotide bases. Chromosomes may also be mutated by duplication or inversion (switching), which are exactly as they imply. In a **mismatch mutation** in a chain of double-stranded DNA, one of the base pairs (adenine to thymine and guanine to cytosine) isn't complementary to the corresponding base in the other chain. A **chain termination mutation** generates a stop **codon** that prevents further synthesis of the polypeptide chain. Other types of mutation include **point mutation** of a single nucleotide, and **missense mutation** of a single base substitution that changes the codon resulting in a different amino acid. A **frameshift mutation** is the addition or a subtraction of a base pair, so coding doesn't read the intended triplet sequence.

These disorders may be genetic in origin, passed down during improper meiosis, or can be the result of environmental factors like radiation or toxic chemical exposure. Genetic deletion disorders include various syndromes that have traits like mental retardation, seizures, and other neurological conditions. Extra genetic material disorders have traits like mental retardation, delayed learning, and behavioral problems.

Sometimes it is hard to determine the disorder and chromosomes involved because they are **multifactorial chromosome abnormalities.** Many disorders that are commonly known today are attributed to a combination of abnormal chromosomes, including Alzheimer's disease, attention deficit hyperactivity disorder (ADHD), depression, schizophrenia, Tourette's syndrome, and even hypertension (high blood pressure). Another type of DNA mutation develops through **mitochondrial inheritance**, when mitochondrial diseases are inherited through the mother. These disorders feature mental retardation and other neurological problems. An ecogenic disorder results from the interaction of common environmental factors with a specific genetic predisposition. Breast cancer is considered an ecogenic disorder because although the BrCa gene is passed on maternally, breast cancer may not develop. Instead, its development may depend on exposure to certain environmental factors.

GENETIC MATERIAL STRUCTURE AND DISORDERS OF INCORRECT MEIOSIS

Deoxyribonucleic acid (DNA) is the hereditary blueprint of each cell and contains a full set of genetic instructions for each cell. Earlier, we discussed cell division through mitosis and meiosis and the function of the organelles within each cell, but what happens in the cell nucleus, which contains DNA within the chromosomes?

Chromosomes are composed of chromatin, which is 40% DNA and 60% protein. Ribonucleic acid (RNA), is also associated with chromosomes. In one chromosome, there are 140 million nucleotides coiled in its DNA—and that is just one chromosome of 46. In a sequence of every 200 nucleotides, the DNA are coiled around eight **histones** to form a nucleosome. These nucleosomes combine to form chromatin fibers, which coil into the supercoils that make a chromosome.

Each person has a specific array of chromosomes, called a **karyotype**. Karyotypes differ among species and sometimes individuals. An individual has 23 pairs of chromosomes that differ in size, centromere position, and staining. As noted before, human disorders can be attributed to an altered number of chromosomes. In a **primary nondisjunction**, chromosomes fail to properly separate during meiosis, causing an additional or deficient number of chromosomes in the gamete (sex cell). In an autosome, a deficient number of chromosomes results in monosomics, that is, fetuses that don't survive. A gain in chromosomes is called a trisomy, and some fetuses that are affected may survive while others don't, depending on the autosome position. Infants with Trisomy 21 or 22 survive into adulthood but with mental retardation and developmental delays, a condition also known

HEMOPHILIA: A GENETIC DISORDER
BRINGS DOWN AN EMPIRE

Hemophilia is an X-linked recessive genetic disorder that causes uncontrolled bleeding in those who acquire it. Today, the condition can be treated with injections of clotting Factor VIII or Factor IX, but at the beginning of the twentieth century, little could be done to help those who inherited the disease.

In the early 1900s, Queen Victoria of England, who carried the gene for hemophilia, passed it on to her granddaughter Alexandra. Queen Victoria's other relatives who were affected by the disease married into the Spanish royal family. Alexandra, meanwhile, married Czar Nicholas II of Russia in 1894. Nicholas already was unpopular with Russia's peasants for many reasons, among them his inexperience and the disparity between the wealth of the royal family and the poverty of most of Russia's citizens.

Nicholas and Alexandra were distressed to find out that their son Alexis bled uncontrollably when he was injured. Desperate, Alexandra turned for help to a mystic named Rasputin. As Alexis underwent treatment by Rasputin's purported therapies, the parents resolved to keep their son's disorder a secret. Unfortunately, Rasputin's presence and perceived political influence over the czar only dismayed the Russian people even further, especially when the czar himself took Rasputin's advice to join the Russian Army at the front during World War I. The people did not understand why or how Rasputin could have such control over the imperial family. After the assassination of Rasputin, the czar resigned his throne. This helped bring about the bloody Bolshevik Revolution, allowing the communists to gain control in Russia. The czar's entire family was executed in 1918, ending the 300-year Romanov

as Down syndrome. Often, this condition is the result of a mother's age. (Although men produce new sperm daily, a woman's ova are the same age she is because a certain number of them are produced before her birth.)

If a sex chromosome has a primary nondisjunction, it fails to separate during meiosis. This can result in a XXX female who is sterile, or a XXY male who is sterile with some female characteristics (which is known as Klinefelter syndrome).

dynasty. Communist Russia became a world superpower. Although originally part of the alliance that defeated Nazi Germany during World War II, Russia became an opponent of the United States afterward. The tension between the countries was referred to as the Cold War, and it continued until the demise of the Communist Party's monopoly on power and the dissolution of the Soviet Union in 1991.

FIGURE 6.2 Queen Victoria (*center*) and Albert Edward Prince of Wales (*right*) pose during a visit to Balmoral Castle by Czar Nicholas II, the Czarina Alexandra Fedorovna, and the infant Grand Duchess Tatiana Romanov.

Other gametes that have no resulting sex chromosome due to improper meiosis are simply deemed "O." If the resulting chromosome is OY, the zygote will not survive, since humans need genes from the X chromosome. If the result is XO, the child will have Turner syndrome, which results in sterility, retardation, and lack of sexual maturity.

If there is improper Y meiosis, the resulting XYY disorder is called Jacob's syndrome. This disorder has been shown to be 20 times more common in men who reside in mental institutions and prisons, but not all men with XYY have behavioral disorders.

GENETIC COUNSELING

The advent of genetic counseling has offered parents and would-be parents the chance to consider and plan their options in regards to having children based on information obtained by genetic counselors. Sometimes

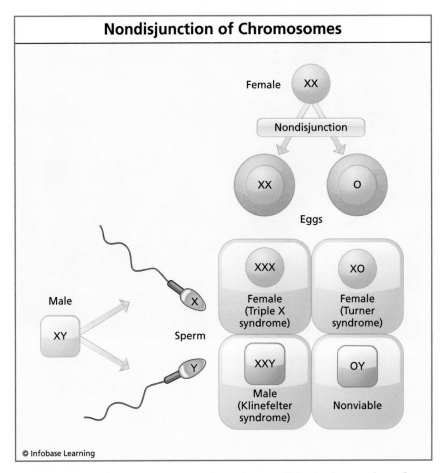

FIGURE 6.3 Nondisjunction can produce abnormalities in the number of sex chromosomes. When nondisjunction occurs in the production of female gametes, the gamete with two X chromosomes (XX) produces males with Klinefelter's syndrome and females with triple X syndrome. The gamete with no X chromosome (O) produces females with Turner syndrome (XO) and nonviable males lacking an X chromosome.

would-be parents want to find out whether a genetic disease in their family history will affect the planned child. Sometimes genetic testing is performed after a child is born with a disability.

The first step performed in genetic testing is a **pedigree analysis** of the known family history. This can be done via interviews and medical records to search for signs of a disorder, but may need confirmation from blood and fluid samples from the parents and relatives. Either based on the genetic analysis or because of other factors, such as the mother's age, a pregnant woman may be classified as being at high risk for a certain disorder. The mother can then choose to have **amniocentesis** of the amniotic fluid in the amniotic sac surrounding the fetus; or she may elect to have **chorionic villi sampling**, which is less risky to the fetus. This sample is taken from the chorion, which nourishes the placenta, and is less invasive. One popular method for mapping the genetic material of an individual's cells is called **FISH (fluorescence in situ hybridization)**. This genetic analysis can be used to identify specific gene locations and helps determine genetic deletions or translocations.

A geneticist is looking for, or at, the karyotype of the fetus, the proper functioning of enzymes, or association with known markers. By studying a fetus' karyotype, a geneticist can detect errors of chromosome deletion, additional chromosomes, improper breaks, or translocated chromosomes. As noted earlier, these types of chromosomal abnormalities are responsible for conditions such as Trisomy 21 or 22 (forms of mental retardation) and other conditions (many of which involve impaired cognitive ability). Improperly functioning enzymes can result in conditions such as PKU or Tay-Sachs disease, while specific markers are noted in conditions like muscular dystrophy, sickle cell anemia, and Huntington disease.

TRANSCRIPTION AND TRANSLATION OF GENETIC MATERIAL

Deoxyribonucleic acid (DNA) is very small, measuring 2 nanometers in diameter, and has a double-helix structure with nucleotide base pairs that point inward. The base pairing is adenine to thymine and guanine to cytosine. The pairing of adenine to thymine will always occur in the same proportion as guanine to cytosine.

When DNA replicates, the DNA double helix opens and the strands separate. In the first step, the helix opens because of the binding of **initiator proteins.** In the second step, DNA itself cannot be **synthesized** (created) on these two exposed strands, but rather needs an **RNA primer**

DNA Replication

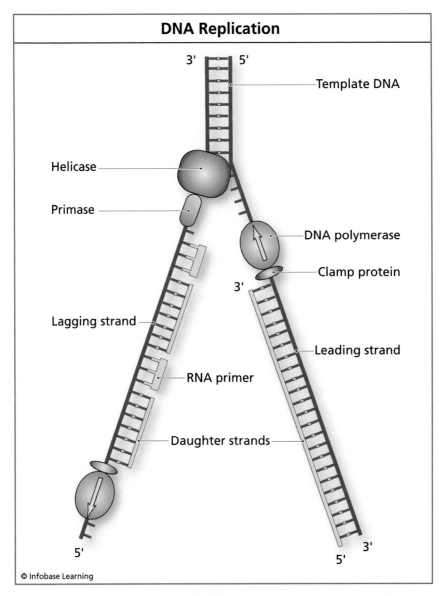

FIGURE 6.4 In DNA replication, the helicase separates the two strands so the DNA polymerase can synthesize new strands. The primase provides replication signals, in the form of RNA primers, for the polymerase, and the clamp protein keeps the polymerase from falling off the DNA. The leading strand requires only a single primer (*not shown*). The lagging strand requires many primers, and the daughter strand is synthesized as a series of DNA fragments that are later joined into one continuous strand.

for replication. In the third step, **DNA polymerase III** binds to the two single strands that were created by the DNA opening up. Complementary sequences of base pairs form on both strands. While one daughter strand is synthesized in one continuous piece, the other daughter strand is synthesized in pieces due to the orientation of the strands that run in opposite directions. In the fourth step, the enzyme **DNA polymerase I** removes the RNA primers and fills in any gaps between fragments. Finally, in the fifth step, another enzyme called **DNA ligase** ties the fragments to the strand in the daughter strand that isn't synthesized continuously. DNA replication only occurs at specific sites called origins of replication.

Cells use RNA to make protein. The steps in the process to create polypeptide chains, of which one or more of these make up a protein, is described as follows. Together, these two steps are responsible for gene expression.

When DNA is transcribed into a RNA sequence, this is known as **transcription.** This process begins when an enzyme called **RNA polymerase** moves along the strand into the gene. As the RNA polymerase meets each DNA nucleotide, it adds the corresponding complementary RNA nucleotide to the growing **messenger RNA (mRNA)** strand until it reaches a stop signal. **Translation** then begins when **ribosomal RNA (rRNA)** attaches to the start sequence of mRNA. The ribosome reads three nucleotides at a time until it reaches a stop signal, which is followed by the release of a complete protein.

The process of gene expression also involves **transfer RNA (tRNA)** that transports amino acids to the ribosome to help build polypeptides. This tRNA is also responsible for positioning each amino acid in the correct place on the growing polypeptide chain.

Regulating transcription controls gene expression. Transcription can be controlled by regulating promoter access. This means that RNA polymerase must be able to bind to the promoter (a specific sequence of nucleotides), which tells the RNA polymerase where to start transcription on a gene.

The overall development and health of cells and body systems are dependent upon gene expression. The primary function of gene control is to maintain homeostasis, or the maintenance of a constant internal environment. The cell should not respond to the immediate environment around it, but regulate the body as a whole. During human growth and development, many biochemical reactions occur that are regulated by enzymes. Once a change in development happens, enzymes must turn off. Many enzymes are only turned on once for a specific period of time. Cell differentiation is usually the last step in the developmental process. If enzymes remain turned on any longer than needed, this would disrupt events that follow! For example, late in development, certain enzymes are turned on that create fingers from the webbed skin of the hand. Genes control when this enzyme is activated and for how long. In another important example, genes also assist in the development of **stem cells,** the precursor cells that develop into many differentiated tissues like red blood cells, skin, bone, or nerve cells.

Gene expression can also be post-transcriptional. When a gene is transcribed, it has **exons**, coding sequences of amino acids in proteins as well as **introns**, that is, non-coding DNA. Introns, which comprise about 90% of transcript DNA, are removed after transcription via **RNA splicing**.

Another factor that affects gene expression is the stability of mRNA transcripts in the cell cytoplasm. This stability has a major impact on regulatory genes. As one can see, the family traditions that we pass on in our genes can be either beneficial or harmful to us as well as our own descendants.

Modern Scourges: The Threats of Cancer and HIV/AIDS

CANCER: THE WAYWARD CELL

Cancer cells are transformed normal cells that undergo uncontrolled growth and division that is caused by the alteration of the cells' growth-regulating mechanisms. Cancer cells, also known as neoplasms (a Latin word for "new growth"), can arise from a genetic disposition to the disease or exposure to ultraviolet light, X-rays, viruses, and chemical carcinogens. Cancer cells evade the immune system and spread (metastasize), and can cause **malignant** tumors.

Cancer is the second leading cause of death in Western countries, after heart disease. One in three people will get cancer during their lifetimes, and one in five will die from it.

Research suggests that neoplasms may grow several millimeters, and then lie dormant for months or years. At some point, they emit a substance that causes the creation of blood vessels. These vessels have leaky walls that allow cancer cells to metastasize. A **benign neoplasm** resembles the normal cells it originated from and does not metastasize. However, cells that show abnormal maturation and appearance frequently progress to cancer.

Cancer can affect any part of the body. There are several types of cancer. These types are related to a cancer's location or cell type. Most human cancers are **carcinoma**, which originate in the epithelial tissue. **Sarcoma** is the cancer of connective tissues or muscles. **Melanoma** is cancer of the

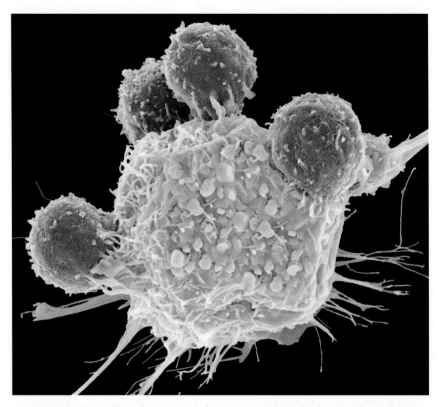

FIGURE 7.1 This colored scanning electron micrograph shows T lymphocyte cells (*in pink*)—white blood cells that recognize and bind to a specific site (antigen) on the surface of cancer cells—attached to a cancer cell. Once attached, some T lymphocytes signal for other immune system cells to eliminate the cell. The genetic changes that cause a cell to become cancerous lead to the presentation of tumor antigens on the cell's surface.

pigmented cells of the skin, and can arise from prolonged, unprotected ultraviolet light exposure. Cancer is also divided into categories of primary (the organ affected is the first organ to have cancer), secondary (the second site affected by cancer), tertiary, and so on. There is more than one cancer classification system, and cancer is generally described in stages. Stage I cancer is localized to one small area that has not spread to other parts of the body via the lymph system. Cancer Stages II and III affect certain numbers of lymph nodes and regions with definitions of how far into neighboring tissues the cancer cells have traveled. Stage IV is the final stage of cancer in which multiple body organs are affected by its spread.

Cancer's Attack and the Body's Defense

The body's T cells are able to recognize tumor-specific antigens and tumor-associated antigens. The **tumor-specific antigens** are unique to cancer cells and are induced by viruses and chemical and physical carcinogens, such as ultraviolet light. However, most cancer antigens are **tumor-associated antigens**. Interestingly, these antigens are not unique to cancer cells. Normal cells express tumor-associated antigens during fetal development, and some are expressed at low levels after birth. However, high levels of these antigens stimulate the immune system. The **oncogenes,** which encode tumor-associated antigens, have the potential to cause cancer.

Cancer cell antigens induce antibody-mediated and cell-mediated responses. Macrophages produce tumor necrosis factors (TNFs) and other cytokines to stop tumor growth. T cells are also activated, which produce interferons, which have an antitumor effect. T_c cells directly attack cancer cells, and produce interleukins. These, in turn, attract and turn on the

FACTS ABOUT CANCER CELLS

Although cancer is a prevalent disease, there are many misconceptions about it. Here are the facts:

- You can get cancer from mutations caused by the human papillomavirus that is spread through sexual contact.
- One in three people will get cancer in their lifetime.
- Smoking and drinking cause serious addictions, and you may not be able to quit in time to prevent the occurrence of cancer.
- Traditional medicine has access to the drugs and therapies used to treat cancer, and tracks cases nationwide; however, alternative medicine therapies may be able to play a role in cancer treatment.
- Effective treatments and surgery can cure many cancers or at least increase the number of quality years a person can live with the disease. Many cancers today have a 70% or higher cure rate in both children and adults. However, death rates from certain cancers remain very high, including rates for lung, liver, and pancreatic cancers.

natural killer (NK) cells and macrophages. However, sometimes cancer cells multiply uncontrollably due to the following conditions: Either cancer cells block T_c action or they decrease expression of class I MHC, which the T_c cell surface membrane molecule needs in order to activate.

The Genetic Mastermind of Cancer Cells

Oncogenes are the cancer-causing genes involved in the development of the disease. At least one, but perhaps several, oncogenes cause changes in **proto-oncogenes**, which are normal genes. This can be accomplished through mutations caused by a virus that may look like a proto-oncogene. Cell proliferation is triggered by growth factors that cause substances to be released, among other actions. Of the known proto-oncogenes, many of them code for growth factors and related substances. If an oncogene mutates or expresses incorrectly, the cell misinterprets the signal, causing growth and division. Sometimes, an oncogene can be permanently switched on.

In addition to proto-oncogene mutation, half of all cancers are due to the mutation of the tumor suppressor genes, which block cell division. There are 100 known oncogenes and 15 tumor suppressor genes. Cancer usually involves both types of mutations and goes through several steps.

Other genetic components that contribute to the development of cancer are thought to include chromosomal translocation and incorrect activation of the enzyme responsible for telomere maintenance.

How Are Cancers Treated?

In traditional medicine, cancer can be treated with chemotherapy (drugs), radiation, or surgery. The problem with most current chemotherapy and radiation therapies is that they kill both cancer and normal cells, and may bring further harm to the patient. Therefore, medicine needs to develop more targeted therapies. Some current advanced therapies include:

- Engineering cancer cells to secrete cytokines that will trigger an immune response.
- Chemotherapy with monoclonal antibodies (antibodies made by identical immune cells; they are clones of a unique parent cell) that block growth factors. Monoclonal antibodies stick to target cancer cells and stimulate the body's own immune response to attack. (An example of this is the breast cancer drug Herceptin.)

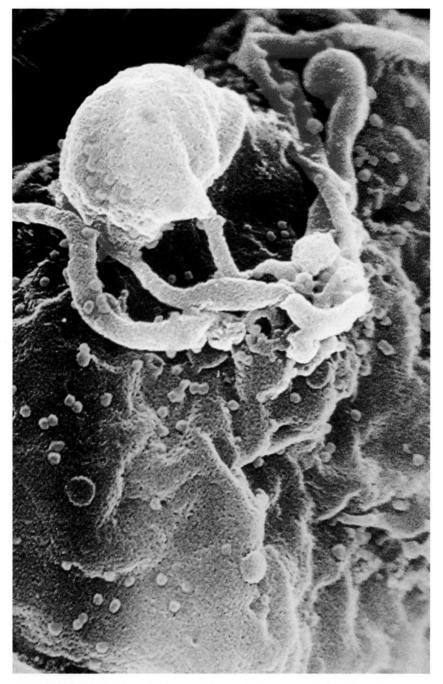

FIGURE 7.2 A scanning electron micrograph shows HIV-1 budding from a cultured lymphocyte. The multiple round bumps on the cell surface represent sites of budding of virus particles.

- Angiogenesis inhibitors that block blood vessel development, so tumors don't have the means to spread and grow.
- Anticancer vaccines that prevent cancer from developing in a person before it occurs; for example, Gardisil, which is used to prevent cervical cancer.

Identification of the disease and the most effective treatment for it can be found through the use of DNA microarrays, which use DNA from blood on slides or microchips for analysis.

HIV AND AIDS: A MODERN PANDEMIC

Acquired immunodeficiency syndrome (AIDS) is the fourth leading cause of death worldwide. This disease, which is caused by the human immunodeficiency virus (HIV), is thought to be transferred from SIV, a similar disease that may have jumped from monkeys to humans in Africa as far back as the 1950s and perhaps even as far back as the 1920s.

There is a possibility that SIV was transferred to humans by way of polio vaccines back in the day when screening of vaccines for potential viruses was not performed. (Polio vaccine cultures contained monkey kidney cells in order to grow the pathogen for use in the vaccine.)

It wasn't until 1983 that HIV was isolated, and, in 1984, its association as a cause of AIDS was established. This once relatively obscure disease, first attributed to gay Haitian men in bathhouses in New York and intravenous drug users in 1981, has reached pandemic proportions. As of 2009, an estimated 33 million people were living with HIV in the world. More than 26 million lives have been lost to AIDS, with more than 3 million new cases yearly. Projections by WHO and a joint United Nations program estimate that there will be 70 million deaths from AIDS by 2020.

HIV Transmission and Infection

Human immunodeficiency virus, the pathogen responsible for AIDS, is transmitted by sexual intercourse and tainted blood. It is mostly spread by men who have participated in homosexual activity or have used illegal intravenous drugs, but it can be spread through sexual activity between an infected man and women, too. Ten percent of AIDS patients are children who are born to AIDS mothers, who pass on the virus via breastfeeding.

FACTS ABOUT HIV/AIDS

The scientific discovery of AIDS was made in 1983, and yet there remain many misconceptions about the virus and people who have it. Here are some facts:

- Only 15% of those infected with HIV show symptoms, and may have the infection for years before becoming more ill with AIDS. Otherwise seemingly healthy and athletic people can have HIV

(continues)

FIGURE 7.3 When AIDS was first discovered in 1983, misconceptions about the disease quickly spread and many people worried about having contact with people who were infected. Here, teenage AIDS victim Ryan White—with mother Jeanne (*left*) and attorney Charles V. Vaughan (*rear*)—talks to the press after a judge threw out a temporary injunction barring him from attending classes at Western Middle School near Kokomo, Indiana, on April 10, 1986. Ryan, a hemophiliac who contracted the virus through a blood transfusion, died of AIDS on April 8, 1990.

(continued)

infection or AIDS, as shown by professional basketball star Irving "Magic" Johnson and Olympic diver Greg Louganis.

- You can't catch HIV or AIDS from someone through casual social contact, kissing, hugging, mosquitoes, or sharing a glass or silverware.
- Although the chance of HIV or AIDS infection is greater with repeat exposures and some people may appear immune, it is possible to catch HIV from only one exposure.
- You can catch HIV or AIDS from heterosexual intercourse with a person who is infected with HIV or AIDS. It is possible to contract HIV or AIDS from blood transfusions or organ transplants if proper screening techniques are not used (which is more likely to occur in other countries).
- Effective treatments are now available for HIV that prolong the period before it develops into AIDS. Many people have lived successfully with HIV for decades.

Safeguards to public health include the promotion of "safe sex" practices, which include the use of condoms during sexual intercourse, and the screening of blood donated to blood banks.

The discovery of HIV led to increased knowledge about cells and virus functions. The HIV virus infects **dendritic cells** in the mucus membranes, which transmit the virus to the lymph nodes. Protein or HIV attaches to **CD4+T cells** and to another receptor that usually binds cytokines. HIV kills the CD4+T cells. T_c attacks HIV, limiting viral replications and slowing the disease. However, HIV eventually wins.

Only about 15% of people with HIV infection have symptoms, which include mild flu-like symptoms like fever and muscle aches. The virus may replicate for years before more severe symptoms, including swollen lymph nodes, night sweats, fever, and weight loss, become apparent. AIDS can cause a variety of unusual and specific illnesses, including AIDS dementia complex, Kaposi sarcoma (a cancer that features vivid, large purple spots on the skin), rare cancers, and opportunistic infections (sicknesses that arise because of a weakened immune system).

Current Treatment of HIV and AIDS

The first drug that was developed for the treatment of AIDS was azidothymidine (AZT), which is still used today to delay the onset of AIDS. Other drugs used to treat HIV and AIDS include protease inhibitors and reverse transcriptase inhibitors. Protease inhibitors block proteases, which are protein-cutting enzymes that allow HIV to enter cells. Reverse transcriptase inhibitors block a DNA polymerase enzyme that transcribes the RNA genome into DNA. When HIV infects a person's CD4+T cell, it copies its genetic code into it. Both protease inhibitors and reverse transcriptase inhibitors are responsible for slowing the replication of DNA from HIV, which is the virus responsible for the development of AIDS. People with AIDS, as well as cancer, are sometimes treated with bone marrow transplants to help stimulate new blood cell growth.

Although there have been several attempts to create an AIDS vaccine, research has been difficult because of mutations in the virus and the lack of an effective animal model to test potential vaccines. It is obviously unethical to use people for such a purpose.

8

Cell Repair, Replacement, and Death

Each person is programmed to be born, grow and develop from childhood through adulthood, and eventually die. What make us truly human are the experiences and moments along the way. As the smallest unit of the entire human body, each cell also starts out as a new cell arising from an existing one, growing and developing, and eventually dying. So far, we have learned how a cell is made, as well as how it grows and develops. However, what is involved in the aging of cells and their eventual death? Is there a hope for regeneration of cells? Whether or not the fountain of youth is found, what can be done to preserve and prolong the health of cells?

WHAT HAPPENS AS CELLS AGE AND DIE?

Lucky for us, humans do not experience aging all at once, but rather in various stages at varying degrees in the organ systems. Over time, a man between the ages of 30 and 75 will experience a 64% loss of taste buds, a 44% decrease in kidney function, and a 37% loss of spinal nerve function. The nerves will be 10% slower and blood supply to the brain will be 20% less. Even the lungs will experience a 44% decrease in vital capacity. However, the human body is more than prepared to accommodate for these losses in function. Although women experience similar losses in function, on average, women live about 8 years longer than men.

What happens when cells age? Overall, during aging, the homeostatic response to stress decreases in the body. Stress is comprised of both internal and external challenges to the body. It is unknown whether a genetic component is entirely responsible for the aging process. However, the cells that stop dividing early in life are more susceptible to the effects of aging as compared to those that continually renew. For example, the nerve cells of the brain are more likely to show signs of dementia as compared to aging-related breakdowns in red blood cells that renew each day.

Additionally, the cells of older adults appear to divide less rapidly than in a younger individual, barring cancer. This may be related to the fact that aging cells lose the ability to produce active telomerase, which replicates the DNA of the chromosomes. Apoptosis, genetically programmed cell death, is essential for development, but may also later be a factor for aging.

Certain environmental conditions, including ultraviolet light, radiation and toxic chemical exposure, as well as alcohol, tobacco, and other drugs, influence cell aging. Hormonal changes and immune system disorders can lead to increased aging.

Although these factors seem to be stacked against us with no magic elixir for youth in sight, there are things we can do to improve our longevity and the health of our cells.

THE ROLE OF DIET IN CELL HEALTH

Proper food choices in the correct amounts are important to the health of our cells and, ultimately, our lives. The major food groups include fruits and vegetables, proteins, grains and cereals, and dairy. Fats also are included as a small portion of the diet. Carbohydrates are found in grains, cereals, vegetables, and fruits. Aside from the carbohydrates found in "junk food," this group should be a major part of a person's diet (50% to 55%). Proteins, which include meat, fish, nuts, eggs, and dairy products, should compose about 15% of a person's diet. Another 30% of foods rich in fat, such as those found in oils, fish, nuts, and fried foods, should be included in a diet. Those wanting to lose weight need to limit their fat intake, since fats contain twice as many calories as proteins or carbohydrates.

How do these food groups benefit cells? First of all, they provide the energy that a cell needs to survive. The more calories a food has, the greater the amount of energy it provides. Carbohydrates and proteins provide 4 calories per gram of food. Carbohydrates provide much-needed vitamins and minerals. Cells can also use the energy from protein as a fuel source, but the body mainly uses protein for cell structure, enzymes, hormones, muscle, and bone. Proteins in meat and fish, as well as some vegetables and fortified cereals, contain necessary amino acids. When calories are not used, they are stored as fat.

The body cannot make 8 of the 20 amino acids it needs. Therefore, we must consume lysine, tryptophan, threonine, methionine, phenylalanine, leucine, isoleucine, and valine in our diets. Vitamins are also necessary elements in our diet. These include the water-soluble vitamins, the group B vitamins (B_1, B_2, B_3, and B_{12}) and Vitamin C, and fat soluble vitamins, A, D, E, and K. Vitamins function as integral parts of cellular enzymes.

Calcium, phosphorus, sulfur, potassium, chlorine, and sodium are crucial minerals for the human body. Large amounts of calcium and phosphorus are needed to build and maintain bones. Additionally, calcium is needed for the proper function of nerves and muscles. Phosphorus is an important mineral needed for adenosine triphosphate (ATP), which supplies the basic energy for human activity, and nucleic acid. In the proper amount, potassium preserves the acid-base balance and the water balance, in addition to providing proper nerve function. Sodium, together with chloride, is an important acid-base that maintains water balance. Chloride is found in gastric juice, and sodium is important to nerve function by way of sodium channels. Iron is needed for cellular respiration, and is an important part of hemoglobin, which carries oxygen in the cell. Sulfur is an important component of many amino acids. Fluorine is needed to maintain tooth structure, and zinc is a component of certain digestive enzymes and proteins.

Minerals are trace elements needed for various functions, including synthesis of enzymes, proteins, hormones, hemoglobin, and urea formation. They also prevent chromosome breakage. These minerals include iodine, cobalt, copper, zinc, magnesium, chromium, molybdenum, manganese, and selenium.

When we digest food in the small intestine, nutrient-rich blood is transported to the liver. The liver is responsible for many metabolic functions, which include providing quick energy and building complex carbohydrates from sugar. Other metabolic functions of the liver include making proteins from amino acids and storing vitamins and minerals. The liver produces bile salts that help break down fat and monitors the production of cholesterol. Other important duties of the liver include regulating blood clotting and detoxifying alcohol, drugs, and poisons.

After the blood flows through the fine passages of the liver, it is then collected into the hepatic vein, which carries the blood to the heart to distribute needed nutrients via the vascular system to the rest of the body.

THE ROLE OF EXERCISE IN CELL HEALTH

When we exercise, our muscles and, thereby, our cells receive much needed oxygen to function. Many organ systems are improved through regular exercise, including the muscular, skeletal, cardiovascular, lymphatic, and digestive systems. Evidence shows benefits to the integumentary system of connective tissues and skin, as well as improved neurological function, due to the increase in blood flow and oxygen function. The resilience of the immune system is increased and the cardiovascular system and muscles are strengthened. Based on a physician's approval, most adults should participate in about 2.5 hours of aerobic activity per week (or 30-to-45 minutes of activity at least four to five times per week), and strength training exercises (weights and bands) at least twice per week.

OPTIONS FOR FAILED ORGANS AND TISSUES

In certain situations, surgeons are able to graft new tissues or promote the production of new cells through bone marrow transplants or even growing new skin. Sometimes an organ transplant from a donor also is a possibility if there is a good tissue antigen match. Regeneration from existing tissues and creation of new tissue from stem cells are discussed in this chapter. Sometimes surgeons use organs from animals with similar tissue structures, such as valves from pig hearts, when a suitable human donor is not available. Similarly, in certain cases, mechanical alternatives may be used. The first artificial heart placed in a human was the Jarvik-7 in 1981, and newer designs of the artificial heart can be used today in humans in dire need of a new organ.

REGENERATION: THE SUPERPOWERS OF THE HUMAN CELL

As if the wonders of the cell and all it can do aren't enough, there is growing evidence that cells, and even whole body parts and organs, have regenerative properties. This means that when a function or part of the body is permanently lost, the body can produce a replacement for the missing function or part.

Usually, the body tries to adapt in ways to accommodate for a loss. For example, if a person loses a tooth, the other teeth move over some to try to fill the gap left behind to allow proper chewing. If a muscle needs to be surgically removed or relocated, the muscles surrounding the missing one will adapt to allow movement of the limb. When a patient suffers a stroke or a surgeon needs to remove part of the brain, nerves are re-routed to provide function to the lost functions of that area of the brain, at least to the point of heightening nerves for similar functions or senses. (For example, if a person loses their sight, then their hearing and smell senses are heightened.)

Infrequently, regeneration can occur. As a more typical example, a dentist can implant a tooth that was knocked out in the hope that the tooth will "re-attach" to the jaw. Recently, surgeons have successfully performed whole face and entire hand transplants. In 2009 and 2010, unique cases of fingertip regeneration have been reported in both babies and adults following the use of a particular wound powder called MatriStem, which contains **skin basement cells,** the deepest cells of the skin.

While doctors have been successfully reattaching peripheral nerves of severed hands through microsurgery, partial and completely severed spinal cords are a different story. However, there has been progress in research in spinal cord regeneration, primarily through external electrical stimulation in humans. In rats, fibroblast growth factor has been used to rebuild nerve bridges in severed spinal cords. However, these methods have not been totally successful in humans. Regardless, even in nerve cells, which were once thought to have limited plasticity (the ability to change as a result of experiences) past childhood, we are learning of amazing restorative powers.

Unfortunately, research into gene therapy—where an abnormal gene is replaced with a normal one—as well as the rejuvenation of cells via hormone therapy, has not been as successful as hoped. Either the results of these techniques have been short-lived, or resulted in serious side effects, including cancer.

In the future, stem cell technology and other technology may make it possible to regrow entire limbs or restore functions of lost organs and body systems. Stem cells offer the most promise because they can differentiate into many different types of cells. However, there is a drawback. Public perception is that research has focused on fetal stem cells from unborn zygotes. However, this is not always the case. Stem cells can be found in adults in bone marrow and in preserved umbilical cords. Future research may allow greater discovery of cures for diseases and regeneration of tissue from these sources.

FINAL THOUGHTS

When observing the true marvels of the universe, from the far-away galaxies to the majesty of the natural wonders of Earth, one must also remember the phenomenally remarkable cell. We have examined the functions of the organelles, the complex immune response, and the unique genetic ability of cells to replicate. We have examined the threats to the cell as well as provided tips on how to best protect the health of cells and ourselves. The cell is wondrous indeed, and is the basis for tissues, organs, and body systems. For the cell, once only imagined and now seen, is the smallest unit of life—the structure that is responsible for the entire you!

Glossary

acellular   A virus or organism that has no metabolism or respiration

acquired immunodeficiency syndrome (AIDS)   the disease caused by the human immunodeficiency virus (HIV)

active immunity   An immune response that develops when an antigen has been encountered

active transport   Wherein cells must expend energy to move molecules across a cell membrane; occurs when transport protein binds to solute and a second site grabs the phosphate group from ATP

adenosine triphophosphate (ATP)   Biological molecule that provides the cell's fuel

alleles   The forms of genes for a trait

amino acids   The building blocks of proteins

amniocentesis   The examination of amniotic fluid surrounding the fetus to check for disorders

anaphase   The phase in mitosis where chromatids separate at the centromere, with a group of chromosomes migrating toward each pole. During anaphase I in Meiosis I, the homologues separate and are pulled toward the poles; during anaphase II in Meiosis II, the centromeres split and the chromatids move to opposite poles.

angiogenesis inhibitors   The agents that are used block blood vessel development

antibodies   Proteins that are specific to certain antigens to help fight infection

antigenic determinant   The area of an antigen on which an antibody binds

antigens   Molecules located on the surface of germs, cancer cells, pollens, house dust, and even cells of transplanted organs

antihistamines   Medicines that block the release of histamine

antiseptic   sterile and free from contaminants

autoimmune disease   When the body cannot distinguish between its own cells and that of a foreign invader

autosomal dominant inheritance   A basic pattern of inheritance where a defect in only one of the two alleles (forms) of a gene leads to a disorder that is from one parent; also known as a "gain of function"

autosomal recessive inheritance   Where a defect in both alleles of a gene leads to a disorder; an affected person must have inherited a defective allele from each parent. This produces a "loss of function" because a loss of both copies is needed to manifest a disorder.

axon   The part of a nerve cell that sends signals

bacteria   One-celled microorganisms that are prokaryotic and mostly heterotrophic; they can be cocci, bacilli, spirilla, vibrio, and spirochete in shape.

B cell   A lymphocyte that originates in blood marrow and matures into plasma cells

benign neoplasm   Resembles the normal cells it originated from and does not metastasize

binary fission   One cell divides into similar cells when circular DNA replicates with the formation of a transverse wall afterward

blastocoel   The hollow, fluid-filled center of the blastocyst produced by fertilization

blastocyst   Ball of cells

cancer   A cell with abnormal cell-cycle control that will divide continuously

carbohydrates   The group of foods that provide support and energy to cells; these organic compounds include sugars, starches, celluloses, and gums.

carcinoma   Cancers that originate in epithelial tissue

CD4+T cells   The helper T cells that bind to antigen presented by B cells; AIDS patients lose these.

cell membrane   Also called plasma membrane, the outer wall of the cell that interacts with the surrounding environment; it is selectively permeable through its lipid bilayer.

cells   Basic building blocks of all living organisms

cell surface marker   The body's recognition of self, such as via the A, B, and O blood groups, versus what is foreign

cell theory   Theory that states that all organisms are composed of cells and that all cells are produced by other cells

centrioles   Parts of the chromosomes that migrate to the poles during prophase in cell division with the formation of spindles between the centrioles

centromeres   Constricted regions of chromatids; the centromere is located near the nucleus and contains centrioles that are important to mitosis.

chain termination mutation   Generates a stop codon that prevents further synthesis of the polypeptide chain

chemokines   A group of cytokines that includes interleukins; important for transmitting signals to other cells for migration during the immune response; they are also important to inflammatory response, and may be responsible for signaling cancer cells to metastasize.

chorionic villi sampling   A sample taken from the chorion, an organ that nourishes the placenta, to test for fetal disorders; this method is less invasive than amniocentesis.

chromatids   One of two sister chromatids that contain identical, double-stranded DNA sequences; together the sister chromatids comprise a chromosome.

chromatin   The complex made up of 40% DNA and 60% protein that makes up eukaryotic chromosomes; chromatin fibers are coiled into supercoils make up a chromosome.

chromosomes   Structures that are composed of supercoils of chromatin, which is 40% DNA and 60% protein

cilia   Hairs that are on the outside of cells that provide movement

codon   A triplet of mRNA nucleotides

complement proteins   These float in plasma in their inactive form and help other defenders of the immune system

cristae   The highly folded inner membranes of the mitochondria that contain enzymes that makes ATP

cytokines   Signaling molecules in the immune system

cytokinesis   An action that produces two daughter cells during telophase in mitosis; during meiosis, cytokinesis occurs during telophase II when nuclei form at the poles and four sets of haploid daughter chromosomes are produced.

cytoplasm   The interior of the cell

cytoskeleton   The skeleton of a cell; includes cilia, flagella, and centrioles; may be formed from actin filaments, microtubules, and intermediate filaments.

deletion   A mutation that arises from the loss of part or an entire chromosome or a loss of DNA nucleotide bases

dendrite   The part of the nerve cell that receives signals

dendritic cell   A cell with branched extensions to convey impulses; it processes antigen material.

deoxyribonucleic acid (DNA)   Nucleic acid that stores hereditary information in cells

diffusion   A method of passive transport in which particles move from an area of higher concentration to an area with lower concentration to create equilibrium

diploid   Having 46 chromosomes in each cell

DNA ligase   An enzyme that joins fragments to the strand during DNA replication

DNA polymerase I   Removes RNA primers and fills in the gaps between fragments during DNA replication

DNA polymerase III   Binds to the two single strands of DNA to catalyze the formation of complementary sequences on two strands at a time

ectoderm   During the gastrulation phase of development, the outer layer of the three-layered organism

endocytosis   A process by which cells absorb molecules (e.g., proteins) by engulfing them

endoderm   The small cluster of cells of the three-layered organism that becomes the anus during the gastrulation phase of development

endoplasmic reticulum (ER) The largest of the internal membranes that are the cell's own circulatory system; it consists of rough endoplasmic reticulum and smooth endoplasmic reticulum.

endospore A resting cell formed from bacteria that can remain dormant for a very long time, even in conditions like extreme dryness or high temperatures

endotoxins In Gram-negative bacteria, endotoxins are contained in cell walls that are released from dead bacteria. When endotoxins bind to the host's macrophages, widespread symptoms such as the resulting fever, are felt by the infected person. Unlike exotoxins, endotoxins cannot be destroyed by heating.

enzymes Biological catalysts that increase the rate of a chemical reaction in the body

equilibrium The balance within the cell

erythrocytes The red blood cells containing hemoglobin that carry oxygen

eukaryotic cells Cells that contain organelles and nuclei; they are found in plants, animals, protists, and fungi.

exocytosis The process by which hormones, neurotransmitters, digestive enzymes, and other substances are secreted

exon The coding sequence of amino acids in proteins

exotoxins These are secreted by some living bacteria and are responsible for causing the symptoms of an illness

fertilization When a sperm successfully enters an egg to begin the development of a zygote

flagella Tail-like appendages of cells that are part of the cytoskeleton that allow movement

fluorescence in situ hybridization (FISH) A type of genetic analysis that is used to identify specific gene locations, and helps determine genetic deletions or translocations

founder effect A defective allele that is found more frequently in descendants of a specific population than in the general population

frameshift mutation The addition or a subtraction of a base pair of a nucleotide, so coding doesn't read the intended triplet sequence

fungi (fungus) Plantlike organisms but without chlorophyll; they live as parasites and saprophytes; most have stalks called hyphae and some reproduce by producing spores while others reproduce sexually.

gastrulation The phase of embryonic development in which the ball of cells becomes a three-layered organism, with ectoderm, endoderm, and mesoderm

gene The hereditary information of a cell with a specific nucleotide sequence in DNA or in RNA in some viruses; in humans, genes are located in chromosomal DNA, and in some mitochondrial DNA.

genetics The study of genes and inheritance in living organisms

germ theory This theory states that disease is caused by microorganisms that invade the body.

Golgi apparatus An organelle that works with the endoplasmic reticulum to collect, package, and deliver protein molecules; it contains Golgi bodies (flattened membrane sacs) and lysosomes.

Gram-negative bacteria The group of bacteria that stains negative on Gram staining (pink or red color)

Gram-positive bacteria The group of bacteria that stains positive on Gram staining (purple-blue color)

Gram staining A technique used to identify two groups of bacteria by staining of peptidoglycan

granzymes These enter into target cells to start programmed cell destruction

haploid Cells that have half of the chromosomes of the parent cell

helper T cells Also known as CD4+T cells; these are the cells that bind to antigen presented by B cells; AIDS patients lose these.

hemoglobin Red blood cells that carry oxygen

histamines Chemical alarm signals that are secreted by mast cells during an allergic response

histone proteins around which DNA coils to form a nucleosome

homeostasis The proper balance of functions in the body; the liver is an important organ for maintaining homeostasis.

hormones Chemical messengers that are produced in one part of the body and transported to another where they signal cells to, in turn, alter their metabolism

human immunodeficiency virus (HIV)   The virus that is responsible for the disease AIDS; it is spread through sexual contact, blood transfusions, and syringe sharing among drug addicts.

human papillomavirus (HPV)   The virus that is responsible for certain warts and certain cancers, such as cervical cancer

immune system   (or **lymphatic system**) The lymphatic vessels, lymph nodes, thymus, tonsils, and spleen that work in conjunction with the circulatory system to transport extracellular fluid; the lymph organs aid in immune defense against microbial infection and cancer.

initiator proteins   The binding of these precedes the opening of the DNA helix during the replication process

innoculation   The introduction of a pathogen or antigen into a living organism to stimulate the production of antibodies

interferons   Proteins that are activated by virus-infected cells; they kill the infected cell and then help neighboring cells by diffusion.

interleukins T_c cells directly attack cancer cells and produce these chemokines; these turn on natural killer cells and macrophages.

interphase   The period a cell is in when no cell division occurs; these phases of interphase include G_1 phase, then the S phase, and finally, the G_2 phase.

introns   The non-coding DNA in proteins

karyotype   A specific array of chromosomes that differs among species and sometimes individuals

killer T cells   Also known as T cytotoxic (T_c) cells; these lymphocytes work to destroy cancer cells.

lipids   Store energy and provide the structure of cell membranes; this class of organic compounds includes fats, waxes, and oils, and cannot be dissolved in water.

lymph   The fluid derived of blood plasma that contains white blood cells

lymphocytes   The white blood cells that govern immune responses

lysosomes   Vesicles formed from the Golgi apparatus that contain enzymes that digest worn-out organelles and wastes

lysozymes   Enzymes found in tissues and body fluids that attack the cell wall of Gram-positive bacteria

macrophages   Phagocytic cells that ingest bacteria; they also produce tumor necrosis factors and other cytokines to stop tumor growth.

malignant   Cancerous

mast cells   Cells that are activated during an allergic response to put out chemical alarm signals called histamines

meiosis   The division of cell gametes that results in haploid cells, a process consisting of two stages: meiosis I and meiosis II

melanoma   Cancer of the pigmented cells of the skin that can arise from prolonged, unprotected ultraviolet light exposure

memory cells   These cells form an imprint of the reaction to an allergen that was encountered previously and launch a stronger response the next time the allergen appears.

mesoderm   The middle layer of the three-layered organism during the gastrulation phase of development

messenger RNA (mRNA)   The RNA is transcribed from DNA, which specifies the amino acid sequence of a protein until it reaches a stop signal.

metaphase   In mitosis, the phase of cell division when spindle fibers attach to kinetochores. In meiosis I, the homologues move to the center of the cell during metaphase I. In meiosis II, the spindle fibers bind to centromeres and the kinetochores move toward opposite poles in metaphase II.

MHC antigens   Major histocompatibility complex antigens; they are responsible for graft rejection.

mismatch mutation   This can occur in a chain of double-stranded DNA; one of the base pairs isn't complementary to the corresponding base in the other chain.

missense mutation   The single base substitution that changes the codon, resulting in a different amino acid

mitochondria   The powerhouse of the cell; this organelle converts the chemical energy of food into the chemical energy of ATP.

mitochondrial inheritance   When mitochondrial diseases happen via maternal inheritance

mitosis   The period of cell division of all cells except sex cells; it occurs in the following stages: prophase, metaphase, anaphase, and telophase.

molecule   The smallest part of a substance formed when two or more atoms are joined together chemically

monocytes   White blood cells that become macrophages

morphogenesis   During development, the process that causes cells to develop a certain shape, such as the bulging of cells in the brain area that will become the eye

multifactorial chromosome abnormalities   Disorders attributed to a combination of abnormal chromosomes; these disorders include Alzheimer's disease, attention deficit hyperactivity disorder (ADHD), depression, schizophrenia, Tourette's syndrome, and hypertension.

muscular system   Skeletal muscle, cardiac muscle, and smooth muscle that produces body movement

natural killer cells (NK)   These cells assist nonspecific and specific immune responses by releasing certain enzymes called cytokines, perforins, and granzymes

neuron   Nerve cell that contains dendrites and axons

neurotransmitters   Chemical signals used by neurons to bridge a synapsis

neutrophils   White blood cells that eat bacteria

nuclear envelope   Two phospholipid bilayer membranes that surround the nucleus

nucleic acids   Macromolecules that house the cell's hereditary information; the small repeating unit is the nucleotide.

nucleolus   The site where rRNA and protein are synthesized

nucleus   The central part of the cell where the nucleic acids are located; plural is *nuclei*

oncogenes   These encode tumor-associated antigens

organ systems   Groups of organs that work together to perform specific activities in the body, including the circulatory, digestive, endocrine, integumentary, lymphatic/immune, muscular, nervous, reproductive, respiratory, skeletal, and urinary systems

organelles   Structures in the cell's cytoplasm that carry out the activities of the cell

ovum   Human egg cell; plural is *ova*

parasites   Unwelcome guests that invade and make their homes in living hosts

passive immunity   The immunity that is provided to a fetus through the mother's immune system response

passive transport   The diffusion of a substance through a cell membrane without the input of cellular energy

pasteurization   The process used to kill organisms in food; it was developed by Louis Pasteur.

pathogen   A disease-causing organism

pedigree analysis   The examination of a record of the family history

perforins   These destroy target cells by poking holes in the surface and allowing granzymes to enter, which initiate programmed cell destruction

peroxisome   Vesicle that has enzymes that catalyze the removal of electrons and hydrogen atoms

phagocytosis   A type of cell death carried out by organelles and certain cells

phenotype   The physical or visible trait that each genotype determines

plasma   The fluid portion of blood where red blood cells, white blood cells, and platelets are suspended

point mutation   The mutation affecting a single nucleotide

primary nondisjunction   When there is failure to properly separate in meiosis, causing additional or deficient number of chromosomes in the gamete (sex cell)

prokaryotic cells   Single-celled organisms without distinct nuclei; for example bacteria.

prophase   The period in mitosis when the nuclear envelope and nucleolus disappear, and chromatin becomes chromosomes; in meiosis I, prophase I begins the process of sex gamete division; during meiosis II, the chromosomes condense and the nuclear envelope breaks down, but DNA does not replicate during prophase II.

proteins   Large complex organic compounds of amino acid subunits that are involved in many cellular activities, providing structure and assisting in chemical reactions

protists   Simple, unicellular eukaryotic microorganisms, many of which cause parasitic diseases in their hosts

proto-oncogenes   A gene that normally carries out cell division

protozoa   Unicellular protists

receptor proteins   Killer T cells that have receptor proteins on the surface of their cell membranes that recognize bits of viral protein on the surface of infected cells and then puncture the cell membranes to kill those cells

respiratory system   Lungs, trachea, and airway that capture oxygen and exchanges gases

Rh (rhesus) factors   Substances found on the surface of red blood cells that cause a strong reaction in individuals who lack the substance on the surface of their red blood cells; it typically refers to antigen D.

Rh incompatibility   Occurs when Rh factors of a mother and father influence the Rh of a baby; this causes a reaction involving Rh antibodies in subsequent babies.

ribonucleic acid (RNA)   The nucleic acid responsible for making proteins

ribosomal RNA (rRNA)   Translation begins when this attaches to the start sequence of mRNA

ribosomes   These cover the surface of rough endoplasmic reticulum; they are responsible for translating RNA copies of genes into protein.

RNA polymerase   Transcription is started by this enzyme, which moves along the strand into the gene.

RNA primer   This is needed for replication during DNA replication

RNA splicing   The removal of introns after transcription

rough endoplasmic reticulum   The organelle that makes proteins for export; the surface is studded with ribosomes that translate RNA copies of genes into protein.

sarcoma   Cancer of connective tissues or muscles

selectively permeable   Allowing certain chemicals in and out

sex-linked inheritance   A form of inheritance of genes coded on sex chromosomes from both the mother (X-linked inheritance) and father (Y-linked inheritance).

single-strand binding protein   A protein that stabilizes the unwound portion of DNA during replication

skeletal system   Bones, cartilage, and ligaments that protect the body and provide support for structure and movement

smooth endoplasmic reticulum   Organelle that is responsible for lipid and carbohydrate synthesis

somatic cells   Produced through a process of division known as mitosis

sperm   Male sex cells

stem cells   Precursor cells that develop into many differentiated tissues like red blood cells, skin, bone, or nerve cells

swine flu (H1N1)   A recent variant of influenza that was acquired from pigs in Mexico and person-to-person contact; an effective vaccine was developed and administered in 2009.

synthesized   Created DNA molecules from existing nucleic acid

T cell   A lymphocyte that originates in the thymus

telomeres   Repeating DNA sequences on the ends of chromosomes

telophase   During mitosis, the phase in which the chromosomes are at the poles and nuclei form; in telophase I during meiosis I, the individual chromosomes are at each pole, and the cytoplasm divides, resulting in two cells (cytokinesis) with each cell containing half the number of chromosomes. During telophase II during meiosis II, nuclei form at the poles and cytokinesis occurs.

tissue   A collection of closely related cells that serve a specific function

toll-like receptors   Proteins that have an important function in the innate response of the immune system

transcription   When DNA is transcribed into a RNA sequence

transfer RNA (tRNA)   Transports amino acids to the ribosome to help build polypeptides

translation   Refers to the conversion of information that begins when ribosomal RNA (rRNA) attaches to the start sequence of mRNA.

tumor necrosis factor (TNF)   Macrophages produce these to stop tumor growth

tumor-associated antigens   Antigens not unique to cancer cells; normal cells express tumor-associated antigens during fetal development; some are expressed after birth but high levels stimulate the immune system.

tumor-specific antigens   Those which are induced by viruses and chemical and physical carcinogens such as ultraviolet light

urinary system   Kidneys, bladder, and ducts that removes metabolic wastes from bloodstream.

vaccination   The injection of weakened, dead, or similar antigen associated with a disease that causes the body to produce antibodies to the disease

vacuole   An organelle that digests byproducts; it is small or absent in animal cells; it stores chemicals and maintains water balance.

virus   A pathogen that has a nucleic acid and a cell wall that is capable of infecting cells; it cannot live outside a host.

white blood cells   Also called leukocytes, which are cells of the immune system that defend the body

X-linked dominant disorder   A sex-linked inheritance that includes RETT syndrome, which almost exclusively affects girls and may be misdiagnosed as cerebral palsy

X-linked recessive disorder   A sex-linked inheritance that almost only affects sons; almost all daughters of an affected male will be carriers.

zygote   A diploid cell that continues to divide via mitosis

Bibliography

Anthony, Catherine Parker and Gary A. Thibodeau. *Textbook of Anatomy and Physiology*, 10th ed. St. Louis: The C.V. Mosby Company, 1979.

"Bacteria Outnumber Cells in Human Body." National Public Radio's All Things Considered. Available online. http://www.npr.org/templates/story/story.php?storyId=5527426. Accessed March 20, 2011.

"Biology Pages, B cells and T cells." Available online. http://users.rcn.com/jkimball.ma.ultranet/BiologyPages/B/B_and_Tcells.html. Accessed March 20, 2011.

Campbell, Neil A., Lawrence G. Mitchell, and Jane B. Reece. *Biology Concepts & Connections* 3rd ed. San Francisco, Calif.: Benjamin/Cummings, 2000.

"CDC Swine Flu Outbreak." Centers for Disease Control. Available online. http://www.cdc.gov/mmwr/preview/mmwrhtml/mm58d0421a1.htm. Accessed March 20, 2011.

"Estimate of Bacteria in World." *Science Daily.* Available online. http://www.sciencedaily.com/releases/1998/08/980825080732.htm

Johnson, George B. and Peter H. Raven. *Biology Principals & Explorations.* Austin, Tex.: Holt, Rinehart and Winston, 1996.

"Mayo Clinic Exercise Recommendations." Centers for Disease Control. Available online. http://www.cdc.gov/mmwr/preview/mmwrhtml/mm58d0421a1.htm. Accessed March 20, 2011

Oram, Raymond F., Paul J. Hummer, Jr., and Robert C. Smoot. *Biology: Living Systems*, 4th ed. Columbus, Ohio: Charles E. Merrill Publishing Company, 1983.

"Origin of AIDS." University of Wollongong, New South Wales, Australia. Available online. http://www.uow.edu.au/~/bmartin/dissent/documents/AIDS/. Accessed March 20, 2011.

Raven, Peter H. and George B. Johnson. *Biology*, 6th ed. New York: McGraw Hill, 2002.

Solomon, Eldra P., Linda R. Berg, and Diana W. Martin. *Biology*, 7th ed. Belmont, Calif: Brooks/Cole-Thomson Learning, 2005.

United Nations AIDS Programme Statistics. Available online. http://www.unaids. org/en/dataanalysis/epidemiology/2009aidsepidemicupdate/. Accessed March 20, 2011.

"Swine Flu." Your Discovery Channel. Available online. http://www.yourdiscov ry.com/web/people/swine-flu/. Accessed March 20, 2011.

Further Resources

Books

Alberts, Bruce, Dennis Bray, Karen Hopkin, Alexander Johnson, Julian Lewis, Martin Raff, Keith Roberts, and Peter Walter. *Essential Cell Biology,* 3rd ed. London: Garland Science, 2009.

Alberts, Bruce, Alexander Johnson, Julian Lewis, Martin Raff, Keith Roberts, and Peter Walter. *Molecular Biology of the Cell,* 5th ed. London: Garland Science, 2007.

Drake, Richard L., Wayne Vogl, and Adam W.M. Mitchell. *Gray's Anatomy for Students.* Philadelphia: Churchill Livingstone, 2004.

Book Companion Site

Solomon, Eldra P., Linda R. Berg, and Diana W. Martin. *Biology,* 8th ed. CengageBrain.com. Available online: http://www.brookscole.com/cgi-wads worth/course_products_wp.pl?fid=M20b&flag=student&product _isbn_issn=9780495107057&disciplinenumber=22.

Web Sites

Centers for Disease Control: Seasonal Influenza
http://www.cdc.gov/flu/index.htm
    This site provides information about flu basics. It also provides recommendations for vaccinations.

Livestrong.com (Lance Armstrong Foundation)
http://www.livestrong.com/
    This site of bicyclist Lance Armstrong, the seven-time Tour de France winner and cancer survivor, provides nutrition, fitness, and cancer support information.

The Living World
http://www.mhhe.com/biosci/genbio/tlw3/eBridge/Chp4/4_keypoints.mhtml
    The Living World is an essential study partner for cellular biology, reinforcing key points.

Mayo Clinic

http://www.mayoclinic.org

The official Web site of the Mayo Clinic of Rochester, Minnesota, provides information about the medical institution, and offers health information through the Mayo Foundation for Medical Education and Research.

Medicine World

http://medicineworld.org/

Medicine World provides the latest updates in medicine from medical convention presentations and published research.

National Cancer Institute Cancer Staging

http://www.cancer.gov/cancertopics/factsheet/detection/staging

This page of the National Cancer Institute Web site is the fact sheet that provides definitions and explanations of cancer staging.

National Libraries of Medicine MedLine

http://www.nlm.nih.gov/medlineplus/

This Web site is the service of the U.S. National Library of Medicine and National Institutes of Health (NIH), which provides the latest news in medicine, definitions of medical conditions and drug information.

Your Discovery Channel

http://www.yourdiscovery.com

The official Web site of the Discovery Channel provides information about interesting topics in science.

Picture Credits

Index

A

acellularity, 67

N-Acetyl neuraminic acid. *See* Neu5AC

Acinetobacter baumannii, 72

actinobacteria, 71

active immunity, 56

active transport, 18–19

aflatoxin, 76

aging, 100–101

AIDS (acquired immunodeficiency syndrome), 33–35, 64, 96–99

alcohol, 46, 93

alleles, 31

allergic response, 51–54

alternative medical therapies, 93

amino acids, 89, 102

amniocentesis, 87

amoebas, 73

anaphase, 39, 40, 41

anaphylactic reactions, 52, 53, 54

antibiotic resistance, 32, 35

antibiotics, 31–32, 75

antibodies, 35, 54–56

antibody-dependent hypersensitivity, 52

antigenic determinants, 57

antigenic drift and shift, 67, 77

antigens, 54–56, 93

antihistamines, 53, 54

antiseptic techniques, 27

apoptosis, 101

Aristophanes, 26

asthma, allergic, 53–54

ATP (adenosine triphosphate), 11, 14–15, 18–19, 102

attachment proteins, 70

autism, 56

autoimmune diseases, 60–64

autosomal inheritance, 78–80

AZT (azidothymidine), 99

B

B cells, 51, 57, 60

bacteria, 10, 70–73, 77. *See also Specific bacteria*

bacteriophages, 68–69

bee stings, 53

Beijerinck, Martinus, 65

bilateral symmetry, 45

binary fission, 73

Binnig, Gerd, 25

biogenesis, 27

Black Death, 58, 74–75

blastocysts, 41

blastula, 41

blood cells, 20, 24, 25

blood group antigens, 55

botulism, 70, 73

bubonic plague, 58, 74–75

C

calcium, 102

cancer, 47, 91–96, 98, 104

candidiasis, 76

capsid, 66–67

carbohydrates, 11, 13, 101

carcinomas, 91

Casanova, Jean, 63

catalase, 14

CD4+T cells, 98, 99

celiac disease, 62

cell membranes, 15–17

cell theory, 29

cell walls, 72

cell-mediated hypersensitivity, 52

centromeres, 39, 41

cervical cancer, 35

chemistry of cells, 10–11

chemokines, 51

chemotherapy, 94

chickenpox virus, 28, 58

chimpanzees, 19–20

chitin, 74
chloride, 102
chorionic villi sampling, 87
chromatids, 38
chromatin, 30, 37–41, 83
chromosomes, 15, 30, 39–41, 82–86. *See also* Inheritance
circulatory system, 45, 46
clamp proteins, 88
classification, 19
cleavage, 41
Clostridium spp., 35, 72, 73
clotting factors, 51, 84
complement proteins, 50, 51, 52, 55
compounds, 10–11
conjugation, 73
covalent bonds, 11
Crick, Francis, 32
cristae, 14–15
cytokines, 51, 57, 94
cytokinesis, 39, 41
cytoplasm, 11, 30
cytoskeleton, 15

D

Darwin, Charles, 19–20, 36
delayed hypersensitivity, 52
dendrites, 15, 98
dialysis, 17
diarrhea, 73–74
diet, 46, 47, 101–103
differentiation, 41–45, 90
diffusion, passive transport and, 17
digestive system, 45, 47
diphtheria, 70
diploid cells, 30, 36–37
diseases, 26–27, 63
DNA (deoxyribonucleic acid), 11, 15, 20, 32, 83–90
DNA ligase, 89
DNA polymerases, 89
double helix structure, 32
Down syndrome, 84
dysentery, 73

E

Ebola virus, 33–35
ecogenic disorders, 83
ectoderm, 41, 42, 43
egg cells, 7, 10, 21, 36–37, 39–41
elements, 10–11
embryonic development, 41–45

endocrine system, 45, 47
endocytosis, 17–18
endoderm, 41, 42, 43–44
endoplasmic reticulum (ER), 12–13
endospores, 72
endosymbiotic theory, 8–9
endotoxins, 73
energy, active transport and, 18–19
enzymes, 11, 13, 16. *See also Specific enzymes*
epiblast, 41
epidemics, 58
epinephrine pens, 53, 54
escaped gene hypothesis, 68
Escherichia coli, 71
eukaryotes, 7–10, 12–15
evolution, 19–20, 36
exercise, importance of, 46, 103
exocytosis, 17, 18
exotoxins, 73
extraterrestrial origin of life, 8

F

facilitated diffusion, 17
fat, diet and, 101
fever, 52–53
fission, binary, 73
flagella, 15
Flemming, Alexander, 30, 31–32
fluorine, 102
folic acid, 47
Founder effect, 79
Fragile X syndrome, 79
fungi, 74–76

G

gain of function, 78
Galileo Galilei, 23
gametes, 36–37, 39–41
gastrulation, 41–42
gene therapy, 104
genetic counseling, 86–87
genetic engineering, 69, 70
genomes, 21, 32–33
germ plasm theory, 30
germ theory, 27
Giardia intestinalis, 73–74
glycobiology, 20–21
Golgi apparatus, 13–14
gonorrhea, 72
grafting, 55, 103
Gram staining, 72

granzymes, 57
Graves' disease, 60
Guillain-Barré syndrome, 60

H

haploid cells, 30, 36–37, 39
Hashimoto's disease, 62
Hawking, Stephen, 8
helicase, 88
helper T cells, 57
hemoglobin, 63–64
hemophilia, 84–85, 97
hepatitis viruses, 28, 33–35, 58
Herceptin, 94
Hertwig, Oscar, 30
heterotrophs, 71, 74
Hippocrates, 26
histamines, 51
histoplasmosis, 76
HIV (human immunodeficiency virus),
    33–35, 64, 95, 96–99
homeostasis, 10, 48, 89, 101
Homo sapiens, 19–20
homologous chromosome pairs,
    39–40
Hooke, Robert, 24–25
hormones, 11, 16, 44
Human Genome Project, 32–33
human immunodeficiency virus.
    See HIV
human papillomavirus (HPV), 56,
    58–59, 93
humanity, defining, 19–21
humors, 26
Huntington's disease, 78, 87
hydrocephalus, 78–79
hydrogen peroxide, 14
hygiene, importance of, 47
hypersensitivity responses, 52–53
hypoblast, 41

I

immune system. *See* Lymphatic/immune
    system
immunodeficiency diseases, 64
immunoglobulin, 51
inflammatory immune response, 51–54,
    62
influenza virus, 35, 56, 58, 66–67
inheritance, 30–31, 78–79, 82–83
inoculation, 28
integumentary system, 45, 47, 103

interleukins, 51, 57
interphase, 37–38
iron, 102

J

Jacob's syndrome, 85–86
Janssen, Zaccharias, 23
Jenner, Edward, 28
Jesty, Benjamin, 28

K

Kaposi sarcoma, 98
karyotypes, 83, 87
killer T cells, 57
Klinefelter syndrome, 84, 86
Koch, Robert, 27, 28
Koch's postulates, 27

L

Legionella spp., 72
lipids, 11, 13, 16
Lippershey, Hans, 23
Lister, Joseph Jackson, 27
liver, 102–103
loss of function, 79
lupus, 60, 62
lymphatic/immune system
    bacteria and viruses and, 77
    exercise and, 103
    inflammation, allergic response and,
        51–54
    lymphocytes and, 57
    malfunction or failure of, 60–64
    nonspecific immunity and, 50–51
    overview of, 45, 47, 49–50
    specific immunity and, 54–56
    vaccines and, 56
lymphocytes, 49, 57
lysogenic cycle, 70
lysosomes, 13–14
lysozymes, 31–32, 50
lytic cycle, 69–70

M

macrophages, 49, 51, 52, 57, 73, 93–94
malaria, 64, 73, 76, 79
malignancy, 91
Malpighi, Marcello, 23–25
mast cells, 51
MatriStem, 104
meiosis, 10, 30, 39–41, 83–86
melanomas, 91–92

membrane attack complexes (MAC), 51
memory cells, 56
Mendel, Johann Gregor, 30–31
meningitis, 58, 72
mesoderm, 41, 42, 43
metaphase, 39, 40, 41
MHC (major histocompatibility complex) antigens, 55
Micrographia (Hooke), 24–25
microscopy, 23–25
minerals, 102
mitochondria, 14–15, 83
mitosis, 10, 36, 37–39
molecules, 10–11
monoclonal antibodies, 94
monocytes, 50, 52
monosomics, 83
Montagu, Mary Wortley, 28
morphogenesis, 44–45
mRNA (messenger RNA), 89, 90
mucus membranes, 50
multifactorial chromosomal abnormalities, 82–83
multiple sclerosis, 60
muscular system, 45, 47
mutations, 82–83, 94
mycotoxins, 76
myelin, 60

N

natural killer cells, 50, 57, 94
Neisseria spp., 71, 72
neoplasms, 47, 91–96, 98, 104
nervous system, 45, 47
Neu5AC (N-acetyl neuraminic acid), 20–21
neural tube, 42
neurotransmitters, 11, 16
neutrophils, 50, 51
Nicholas II (Czar of Russia), 84
Nocardia spp., 71
nondisjunction, 83–84, 86
nonspecific immunity, 50–51
notochord, 42
nucleic acids, 11, 68. *See also* DNA; RNA
nucleolus, 15
nucleotides, 32
nucleus, 15, 30, 68
nutrition, 46, 47, 101–103

O

Odierna, Giambattista, 23

oncogenes, 93, 94
organ systems, 10
organelles, 10, 12–15, 72
organic compounds, 11
organs, 43–48, 103
origins of life, 8–9
osmosis, 17
ova, 7, 10, 21, 36–37, 39–41

P

pandemics, 58, 74–75
panspermia theory, 8
passive immunity, 56
passive transport, 16, 17
Pasteur, Louis, 27, 65
pasteurization, 27
peanut allergies, 53
pedigree analysis, 87
penicillin, 31–32, 75
peptidoglycan, 72
perforins, 57
permeability, selective, 16
peroxisomes, 14
phagocytes, 18, 50
phagocytosis, 14, 17, 52, 57
phenotypes, 31
phosphorus, 102
PKU (phenylketonuria), 79, 87
plague, 58, 74–75
plasma membranes, 15–17
plasmids, 72
Plasmodium falciparum, 76
Plato, 26
pneumococcal disease, 63
polymerase chain reaction, 88
polypeptides, 89
polysaccharides, 20–21
potassium, 102
potassium channels, 16
pregnancy, 47
primary immune response, 55
primary nondisjunction, 83–84, 86
programmed cell death, 101
prokaryotes, 8–9, 10, 65, 71
promoters, 89
prophase, 38–41
protease inhibitors, 99
protein, dietary, 101–102
proteins, 11, 89–90
protists, 73–74
proto-oncogenes, 94
pseudopodia, 73

psoriasis, 60, 62
Purkyne, Jan Evangelista, 26

R

radiation therapy, 94
receptor proteins, 57
receptor-mediated endocytosis, 17–18
regeneration, 103, 104–105
rejection, 55
Remak, Robert, 26
reproductive system, 46, 47
resistance, 32, 35
respiratory system, 46, 48
RETT syndrome, 79
reverse transcriptase, 68
reverse transcriptase inhibitors, 99
Rh (rhesus) factors, 20, 55
rheumatoid arthritis, 60
RNA (ribonucleic acid), 11, 15, 83, 89
RNA polymerase, 89
RNA splicing, 90
Rohrer, Heinrich, 25
rRNA (ribosomal RNA), 89
Ruska, Ernst, 25

S

sarcomas, 91
scanning tunneling electron microscopes (STEM), 25
schizophrenia, 83
Schleiden, Matthias Jakob, 26
Schwann, Theodor, 26
scleroderma, 62
secondary immune response, 55–56
selective advantage, 79
selective permeability, 16
sex-linked inheritance, 78, 79, 80–81, 82
sickle cell anemia, 63–64, 79, 87
simian immunodeficiency virus (SIV), 33, 96
skeletal system, 46, 48
skin basement cells, 104
sleep, importance of, 46
smallpox, 28, 56, 63
sodium, 16, 19, 102
somatic cells, 36
specific immunity, 54–56
sperm cells, 7, 10, 21, 36–37, 39–41
spinal cord injuries, 104
splicing, 90
spontaneous generation, 8, 26
spores, 75

Staphylococcus spp., 35, 71
stem cells, 21, 90, 105
stop codons, 82
Strasburger, Eduard, 30
Streptococci, 71
structure of cells, 11–17
sulfur, 102
systemic lupus erythematosus, 60, 62

T

T cells, 51, 55, 57, 60, 93
T lymphoctes, 92
taste, sense of, 21
Tay-Sachs disease, 79, 87
telomerase, 101
telophase, 39, 41
tetanus, 58, 72
thimerosal, 56
tissues, 45–48
TNF. *See* Tumor necrosis factors
Toll-like receptors, 51
tools, use of, 19
Tourette's syndrome, 83
transcription, 89
transduction, 73
transformation, 73
translation, 89
transmembrane proteins, 16
transplants, 104
transport processes, 17–19
trisomy, 83–84, 87
tRNA (transfer RNA), 89
trophoblast, 41–42
tumor necrosis factors (TNF), 51, 57, 93
tumor suppressor genes, 94
tumor-associated antigens, 93
tumor-specific antigens, 93
Turner syndrome, 85, 86
twins, 37
Type I diabetes, 60

U

urinary system, 46, 48

V

vaccination, 28, 35, 56, 58–59, 63–64, 66–67, 96
vacuoles, 14
van Beneden, Edouard, 30
van Leeuwenhoek, Antonie, 25, 27
Virchow, Rudolf, 26, 30

viruses, 65–70, 77, 94. *See also Specific viruses*
vitalism, 26
vitamins, 102
vitiligo, 62
von Waldeyer-Hartz, Heinrich, 30

W

Watson, James, 32
Weismann, August, 30

White, Ryan, 97
Wilkins, Maurice, 32
Williams syndrome, 79

X

X-linked disorders, 79–82

Z

zinc, 102
zygotes, 37

About the Author

Ingrid Schaefer Sprague is a medical writer with more than 20 years of experience. The focus of her career has been the medical education of resident physicians. She was the medical editor for the Department of Surgery, Saint Luke's Medical Center of Cleveland under Helmut Schreiber, MD, and for plastic surgeon Bahman Guyuron, MD. Sprague has written medical courses for resident physicians in dermatology, general surgery, genetics, epidemiology, plastic surgery, and psychiatry, and has published and edited peer-reviewed medical journal articles, nursing textbook chapters, oncology patient handbooks, and Web articles. She was a nationally board-certified EMT-A and state-tested nursing assistant, and she has taken coursework in medicine, nursing, and medical technology. Sprague was a disability advocate at the Ohio Second Biennial Governor's Conference for the Disabled in 1986, and a National English Merit Award finalist in 1983. Her interest in education has led to substitute teaching positions in the school districts of Brecksville-Broadview Heights and North Royalton, Ohio. Sprague lives in Cleveland, Ohio.

Dedication

"I dedicate this book to my loving daughter Alana and husband Dean. Their patience and encouragement were a source of inspiration for me to finish this project. I also dedicate it in the memory of my beloved brother David Erwin Schaefer, who was afflicted with muscular dystrophy (spinal muscular atrophy) and was an inspiration to all. Finally, I dedicate this book to the memory of my parents, Erwin and Jean Schaefer, for emphasizing the importance of science."

Acknowledgment

"Thank you to Brecksville-Broadview Heights High School science teacher Robert Berg for providing textbook information."